PRAISE FOR *FROM BAD TO WORSE TO BEST IN CLASS*

"This story is as riveting as it is inspirational. An incredible journey."

—Verne Harnish, Founder of Entrepreneurs' Organization (EO); Author of *Scaling Up*

"A fascinating and funny story that will leave you motivated and set up with ideas to implement in your daily life and company. Hao's book could change your life."

—Cameron Herold, Founder of COO Alliance; Author of *Double Double* and *Meetings Suck*

"In *From Bad to Worse to Best in Class*, we follow Hao on his journey—from a childhood of bad decisions in war-torn Vietnam to being the owner of a successful franchise devoted to quality education in Seattle. The story is at once exciting, encouraging, and eye-opening."

—Kevin Harrington, Original Shark on the hit TV show *Shark Tank*; Inventor of the infomercial; Co-Founder of Pitch Video

"*From Bad to Worse to Best in Class* is a fun, funny, fast-paced adventure that delivers an important message about hard work, true commitment, and using creativity to get the results you want. These are great lessons for all business owners."

—Jeff Hoffman, Partner and Co-Founder of ColorJar, LLC; Author of *Scale: Seven Proven Principles to Grow Your Business and Get Your Life Back*

"Hao is the embodiment of Emma Lazarus's words, 'Give me your . . . huddled masses yearning to breathe free . . .' And here in this shining city on a hill, they can make it. Here they can not only survive but thrive, because here in this land, we are free. *From Bad to Worse to Best in Class* is the story of tenacity, grit, the humility to admit mistakes, and the wisdom to learn and grow from failure; it is an unsung hero's story made possible by the free society. Hao's story teaches us to learn something meaningful from every circumstance, lead with humility every chance we get, and leave a lasting legacy."

—Dan Quiggle, Founder and CEO of the Quiggle Group and America's Choice Title Company; Author of *Lead Like Reagan*

"Most entrepreneurs I know, work with, and invest in have had it way too easy . . . there is *nothing easy* about Hao's story! If you are ready to experience *real* struggle, heartbreaking loss, and ultimate triumph, Hao's book is a *must*-read!"

—Scott Fritz, Founder of Growth Connect; Author of *The 40 Hour Work YEAR*

"By turns funny, poignant, wise, and harrowing, Hao Lam's story is a testament to one man's extraordinary perseverance and infectious optimism. From his childhood in Vietnam, to his nail-biting escape attempts and subsequent capture and imprisonment, to his eventual migration to Canada and, finally, the United States, it serves as a timely reminder of the vital role that immigrants play in the success of modern America."

—Ingrid Emerick, CEO/CFO of Girl Friday Productions

"Never judge a book by its cover. This is not a rags-to-riches story. This is the story of how the pursuit of happiness drives us toward success at all costs. It motivates us. It drives us to crash through all brick walls. It is so much more powerful than riches—as what equals happiness clearly is one of the most desired goals of life. Hao's story explains this with emotion that is raw and daring. When you have come so close to death, as Hao's story dictates, your belief that anything is possible only maximizes."

—Nick Powills, CEO and Founder of No Limit Agency;
Publisher of 1851 Franchise and Estatenvy.com

"This is a truly inspiring book that makes you feel like you are going through it with him. It gives you a new look at life and a greater appreciation for it."

—Evan Hackel, CEO of Ingage Consulting;
Author of *Ingaging Leadership*

"Hao and Lisa Lam prove that the best Americans are first-generation immigrants. Not only did they struggle against great odds to obtain the American dream, they surpassed it by saving others in their family and contributing to their adopted country many times over. This book is a must-read in an era of anti-immigrant bias."

—Roberta Jensen, PhD

"Hao is one of the most interesting, genuine, and happiest people I've ever met. I feel lucky to know him. Read this book to get a glimpse, and know that in real life he's even more amazing!"

—Dr. Stephen Wangen, Co-Founder and CEO of IBS
Treatment Center; Author of *Healthier Without Wheat*

"For many of us the road in business is challenging, but nobody dies in the process of meeting goals. In Hao's journey, dying was certainly a possibility and he met every opportunity with determination and focus. You have only to read this book to understand the value and commitment so many first-generation Americans bring to the tapestry that is our country and our business environment. Let him take you on a journey that will impress you with his accomplishments at every step of his life."

—Sue McNab, semi-retired C-Level Executive,
Executive Coach, and Community Leader

"Hao Lam's book is one of optimism, persistence, and focus. It inspires us to put a plan in place to pursue our dreams, and not be discouraged by hiccups along the way."

—Ivan Ting, Global Chairman of Entrepreneurs'
Organization (EO) 2016–2017

"Hao's journey—from being a smart, resourceful, energetic young man who was attracted to trouble to building an extremely successful business that makes a positive impact on the lives of many—is inspiring. His perseverance through a life of extreme struggles and challenges to become a man admired by many makes him an entrepreneur's entrepreneur."

—Brian Brault, Global Chairman of Entrepreneurs'
Organization (EO) 2017–2018

"There's an old saying: 'It's amazing how lucky you are when you're working your butt off.' Hao's business and personal 'luck' are certainly the result of his working tirelessly, 24-7, as well as working smart, learning from past experiences, and continually searching for new solutions. I've been fortunate to work with Hao for the last few years, sharing ideas, successes, failures, and dreams. Hao has made Best in Class an exciting, fast-growing company while helping thousands of young students improve. His greatest achievement, though, is having a terrific family. I'm proud of Hao and will happily watch his future successes."

—Theodore T. Tanase, Founder of Ensocare

"*From Bad to Worse to Best in Class* is gripping, poignant, and full of hard-earned wisdom. A must-read for aspiring entrepreneurs. After reading this book, you'll find that Hao makes you believe in making the impossible possible."

—James Wong, CEO of Vibrant Cities

"When I met Hao, I was immediately captivated by his enthusiasm, dedication, work ethic, and relentless pursuit for knowledge. Hao's attitude was infectious. He inspired me to grow my law firm and gave me the tools, resources, encouragement, and support to help make my dream a reality. But more than a business mentor and client, I consider Hao a close friend. Every year he invites me (and my entire family) to join him and his team on their corporate retreat. Who invites their attorney? It is just another example of Hao treating his team as family. It's no wonder they are fiercely loyal to him. Hao's perseverance when faced with adversity is a model for us all. One's true character is revealed only when faced with adversity. And Hao does not just survive, he thrives—and in a world full of challenges and tests of his character. I have no doubt he will achieve anything and everything he sets out to do. For people like Hao, 'impossible' does not exist."

—Dan Warshawsky, Co-Founder and Managing Member
Franchise Attorney at Warshawsky Seltzer, PLLC

"Hao Lam's harrowing tale of salvation and redemption is bittersweet and ultimate proof that every soul has the potential of rising beyond their circumstances. In the author's case, he is living the proverbial American dream and demonstrating how 'the rising tide lifts all boats.' From abject poverty, deprivation, near death experiences, and little education, Hao has channeled his painful experiences to create Best in Class, a franchise chain of education centers that has a majority of refugees and immigrants as both its clientele and its operators. There can be no better beacon of light for a world torn apart by the erroneous belief that immigrants can't contribute at the highest levels of society."

—Keith Gerson, CFE President and Chief
Customer Advocate for FranConnect

"*From Bad to Worse to Best in Class* is an amazing and well-told true story of unwavering perseverance to attain a better life. Hao's mindset and purpose are shown clearly throughout his arduous journey, where he continually faces obstacles but remains steadfast in his quest for success and happiness. I have had the privilege of knowing Hao for some time, and for the entire time we've served our local entrepreneurial community together, I've been so impressed by his contagious spirit and perpetual optimism. This story of tribulation and triumph now reveals to me more about why and who Hao is and how truly amazing he is!"

—Mark Sims, CEO and Founder of Fikes Products

"Hao's beautifully written life and love story is a shining example of the power of the human spirit to overcome overwhelming adversity, change and adapt, and ultimately create an intentional new reality that makes the world a better place. Incredibly

inspiring to see the unlimited potential that comes from grit, determination, humility, and true love!"
—Shannon Swift, Founder and CEO of Swift HR Solutions, Inc.

"Reading *From Bad to Worse to Best in Class* is an exercise in perspective for any entrepreneur. When the roller coaster of running a business knocks you down, Hao's story will lift you up! Follow the story of a man who, against all odds, escaped persecution and built a successful business centered on empowering others to achieve greatness in their own lives. You'll laugh, you'll cry, and you'll realize that you, too, are capable of grit and perseverance!"
—Amy Balliett, CEO and Co-Founder of Killer Infographics

"Hao's story is truly an amazing tribute to his character, passion, and dedication to dreaming of a better life for himself and his family. He is a walking example of what 'grit' looks like in a humble and self-effacing package. A stronger yet more humble example of personal determination is tough to find. You will be inspired by what is possible after reading this book!"
—Charles Bender, President and CEO of Skynet Broadband, Biz IT Pros, and West Coast Marketing Group

"*From Bad to Worse to Best in Class* has it all: adventure, hardship, romance, struggle, success, and humor. A true depiction of achieving the American dream."
—Robert Glazer, Founder and CEO of Acceleration Partners; Author of *Performance Partnerships: The Checkered Past, Changing Present & Exciting Future of Affiliate Marketing*

"Perseverance, passion, and people are some of the keys to life and business success. Hao's journey will inspire you to push through whatever you are going through to come out on the other side a winner!"

—Jim Roman, Director of Results at Business Owners Institute

"This is an amazing story about perseverance and overcoming obstacles. Very inspirational and motivational!"

—Jeff Anderson, Founder of the Evergreen Market

"*From Bad to Worse to Best in Class* reveals a personal and intimate story of how determination and appreciation helped Hao and Lisa overcome adversity to find their life's purpose together. Orrin Woodward said, 'Success is assured when a person fears the pain of regret more than the pain of process.' Hao feared that he would regret staying behind in wartime Vietnam, so he risked his life to explore a new beginning. Found within the pages of Hao's book are stories of his painful escape from Communist Vietnam, the process of love and growth with his wife, Lisa, and the challenges he faced to make Best in Class a career success!"

—Andy H. Yeung, CPA, PS

"Hao's story of his efforts to get to America illustrate his unquenchable drive and focus. It's that same drive and focus that has made him one of the most successful entrepreneurs I know. On every front Hao is doing great things: for his customers, his family, his country, and his fellow entrepreneurs. Reading this book is an inspiration. It's also more than that—it's a wake-up call for all of us to strive to do more, to give more."

—Leslie Rugaber, CEO and Founder of Worktank Enterprises

FROM BAD TO WORSE
TO BEST IN CLASS

Dear Evan,

Thank you for the friendship and your guidance. I greatly appreciate your endorsement of this book!

FROM BAD TO WORSE TO BEST IN CLASS

A Refugee's Success Story

HAO LAM

Published by HL Media, LLC, Seattle, Washington
http://www.haolamstory.com

 Edited and Designed by Girl Friday Productions
www.girlfridayproductions.com

Editorial: Anna Katz, Emilie Sandoz-Voyer, Jane Steele, Simone Gorrindo, and Nick Allison
Interior Design: Rachel Marek
Cover Design: Artitudes Design
Image Credits: cover photo © Ellis Kao; interior author photo © Benz Photography

ISBN (Paperback): 978-0-9998919-0-2
e-ISBN: 978-0-9998919-1-9

First Edition

Printed in the United States of America

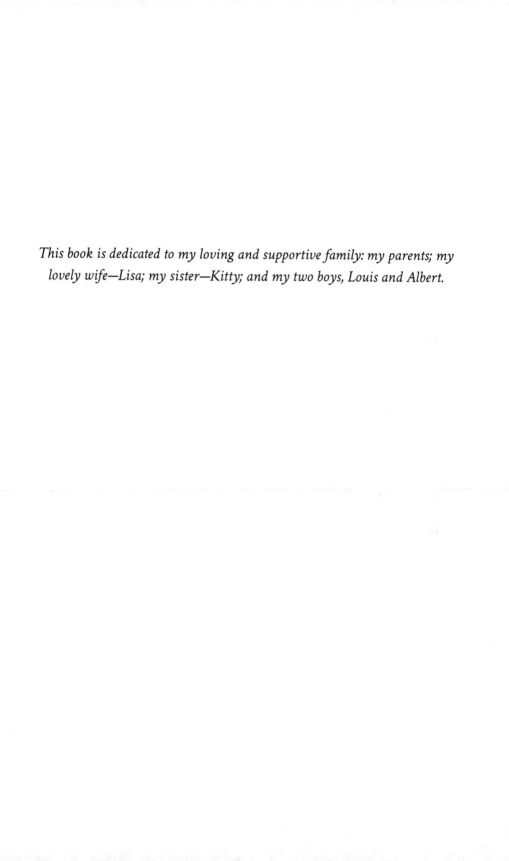

This book is dedicated to my loving and supportive family: my parents; my lovely wife—Lisa; my sister—Kitty; and my two boys, Louis and Albert.

TABLE OF CONTENTS

FOREWORD

In our lives, all too infrequently we come across individuals with the potent combination of great humility, abundant courage, gifted leadership, boundless wit and spirit, and a generous, endearing, giving heart. In the work that I do as a coach and mentor to company CEOs and their leadership teams worldwide, I encounter many superb, gifted individuals—and yet it is extremely rare that any one of them embodies all five of these unique qualities. Hao Lam, however, is one of those few exceptions. And I am glad to call him both a favorite client and a true friend.

In the four years that I have been working with Hao and his team at Best in Class Education Center, Hao has expanded his vision of what success looks like, both for himself and for other entrepreneurs around the world through his increasing leadership role in the Entrepreneurs' Organization (EO). He demonstrates a commitment to perpetual learning, constantly reassessing his business based on his experience with EO and his work with a coach. His current success and his ever-expanding goals underline how far he has come since leaving his native Vietnam twenty-nine years ago, under extreme duress and a perpetual threat of death.

As one of the tens of thousands of boat people fleeing Vietnam after the war, Hao embarked on multiple courageous attempts to find his way to freedom. He was caught several times and incarcerated by the communist authorities of his native land, and he faced imminent death on numerous occasions during his time in official custody.

His continued attempts to escape were a testament to the powerful pull of freedom. Finally, in 1988, he was able to successfully float away from communist Vietnam on a packed fishing boat, where he spent a nightmarish week at sea, drifting east. Storms raged, pirates attacked, food and water were scarce, and, for many, hope faded with each passing day. Repeatedly, the other countries and governments of Southeast Asia—Indonesia, Malaysia, Thailand, and the Philippines—actively turned the floating flock of refugees away, absolutely and coldly unconcerned whether they lived or died.

But hope did not fade for Hao, despite these wretched hardships endured over the course of his repeated attempts to escape Vietnam. Determination replaced despair, and his resilience and leadership skills were forged from the fires of these adversities.

Eventually, Hao and his fellow freedom-seeking exiles landed on the shores of Palawan, in the Philippines, where they were able to gain the respite of temporary asylum. It took all of the patience and gratitude he could muster to withstand and plan through the next year, when the government of Canada sponsored his relocation to British Columbia and humanely offered him a fresh start in life. But that was only the beginning of Hao's story.

Hao's life is truly a profile in courage. In these pages, we find a man persevering against all odds; developing and holding on to a vision for success and eventual redemption; prevailing over an

unending avalanche of obstacles; deliberately planning, execut-
ing, and expanding a life of entrepreneurship and service to new
people all over the globe; and growing a worldwide business that
thrives on building better students, teachers, and entrepreneurs.

Hao has seen the lowest of lows, and he pulled himself up
from the displacement and poverty of his modest refugee roots
with deliberate discipline. His time as a boat person and the rud-
derless journey of those harrowing days crystallized in a burning
desire to grow and succeed that simply would not be extinguished.
These experiences have shaped all of his values, in every aspect
of his remarkable life: as a family man, as a businessman, as a
member and leader of the many communities he serves, and as a
friend and role model to those whose lives he touches.

His journey of inspiration, determination, tenacity, and triumph, told in a remarkable story that continues to unfold, has
the promise of an even brighter future.

I first met Hao at an EO function in Seattle that I was attending with my good friend, Verne Harnish, one of the Founders of
EO, and a respected teacher and educator in his own right. What
first attracted me to Hao was his unrivaled thirst for knowledge
and self-improvement. Already at that time a successful entrepreneur, Hao showed a relentless pursuit of knowledge and pro-
fessional growth.

His life is a persistent quest to make himself a better leader,
manager, and steward of his companies, and to inspire others to
have the same passion for learning and education that he himself
found to be life changing. His core philosophy is that education is
the way to a better life, and that the more you learn, the more you
can earn—and the more you can then give back to those around
you, in time and treasure.

In our work together, Hao has matured into a thoughtful, caring CEO of Best in Class, the supplemental education company that he founded with his wife, Lisa. Hao and Lisa have built an exceptional team at Best in Class Education Center, with a mission to develop an international company that spreads their vision of "the best supplemental education company in the world, which builds the best students and successful franchisees—for successful lives that make a global difference."

So, I invite you to enjoy the ride with Hao, not only in this book—which covers his journey so far—but also into the future, with all the good yet to come for Best in Class. Be a part of the inspirational change and enduring legacy of better students and successful franchisees that Hao Lam is leaving in every corner of the world.

Ron Huntington

Owner of Executive Mentors & Trainers, Seattle, Washington
Founder, Past President, and Emeritus Head Coach of Gazelles International Coaches

PROLOGUE

Most anyone who knew me back in Saigon's District 1 would tell you I was a bad kid.

It's true. I'd steal, skip school, beat up my cousins, and get in fights, not necessarily in that order. Skipping school was the gateway to all other kinds of troublemaking—there's nothing like having a day without structure or adult supervision to get up to no good.

There were plenty of other kids in my neighborhood to play truant with. Sometimes we'd go to an abandoned field next to a park, an oddly shaped piece of land that we turned into a soccer field by throwing some sticks down on either side to serve as goalposts. Then we'd kick off our flip-flops and get a game going. A river ran on the other side of the park, and in the rare moments we weren't taunting one another or screaming for a teammate to pass the ball, we could hear it flowing by. When possible, we'd invite a team from another neighborhood and place a bet. I played rough, focusing on getting the ball where I wanted it even if that required an elbow to the face or a body check. I always kept an eye out for my dad, who could happen by at any moment and chase me down the street toward our house. But he rarely caught me, and no matter the outcome of the game,

I'd always return home with money in my pocket. If we won, we'd keep the money. If we lost, we'd beat the crap out of the other team members, rifle through their pockets while they lay moaning on the ground, and take the money. It only took a team one game with us sore losers for them to learn their lesson, but there were a lot of teams around, and there was always someone willing to play.

Other times, I skipped school so that my friends and I could rob fruit trucks. This was big-time for a twelve-year-old. Whenever we saw a slow-moving truck rumbling by on one of Saigon's dusty roads, its bed stacked full of fruit crates, we'd wait until it passed, then a couple of us would jump on the back while the rest followed behind on the road. Those down below were either the fruit catchers or the lookouts, but I wanted the danger and the glory, so usually I was one of the kids who'd jump up on the bumper and toss down watermelons, pineapples, mangoes, or star apples. Often, we'd sneak away with more than we could carry, leaving split-open fruit and its colorful guts spilling out in a trail behind us. Other times, the truck would grind to a halt, and if we weren't paying attention, we'd get pitched into the truck bed or thrown out onto the road. Then, the driver would climb out and run after us, cursing his head off while we laughed and darted in all directions.

Another favorite activity was "fishing." At low tide, I'd dig up a fat pink worm along the banks of the Calmette River and spear it with a hook attached to a line. Then, I'd perch myself on the Calmette Bridge, weave the line through the wood rails, and lower the writhing worm, waiting patiently for the neighbor's chickens to waddle by, happily clucking while hunting for bugs. Inevitably, a curious chick would notice the worm, and that was that. There wasn't a lot of meat on those young bones, but flame-grilled chick does make a great afternoon snack. The fact that this was stealing hardly crossed my mind.

And sometimes I skipped school simply because I didn't feel like going.

I realize that this may sound surprising, coming from someone who's devoted so much of his life to education. I opened my first education center in Seattle in 1995, six years after I arrived in North America. These centers are my pride and joy, and they provide tutoring for kids, jobs for college students and teachers, and a place for parents who value education to meet. Now, more than twenty years have gone by, and we've multiplied and spread across the United States.

So, you might be wondering how a headstrong, double-crossing, mostly illiterate juvenile delinquent became a community-oriented and upstanding business owner who now values education above just about everything else.

Imprisonment, privation, and near-death experiences can change a person. Falling in love can change a person, too.

CHAPTER 1

Making Trouble

I grew up in Saigon with the war as a kind of background noise, something that was so familiar and ordinary, I didn't even notice it. Most of the fighting itself was happening in the countryside, anyway. Saigon, where I was born in 1968, was always busy with bikes and vehicles struggling for space on the narrow streets. Exhaust, the smells of fish cooking and garbage, and the shouts of vendors filled the air. Young Vietnamese guys walked the streets in uniform, along with a few tall American soldiers in their heavy black boots and army fatigues. Plenty of people in the city were missing an arm, a leg, or an eye, or had puttylike burn scars on their skin. I grew up with the war, the noise, the smells, the colorful faces, the taste of warm dust, and the poverty. It was neither good nor bad—it was my home.

As with most Asian families, multiple generations lived together under our roof—my maternal grandparents, my parents, an aunt and an uncle, my cousins, my sister, and me. My grandmother was the cornerstone of our family. She was a strong, kind, and—I see now—incredibly patient woman who'd raised her own five kids and several of her grandkids. She'd left China at the age of fourteen to escape the Communist Revolution and its aftermath, to pursue adventure and a new life. Like many girls back then, she'd had only two years of education, and yet—or maybe because of this—education was at the top of her priority list.

My grandfather, too, had left China as a teenager. In Vietnam, he'd married a nice young woman who just happened to be my grandmother's best friend. This woman, his first wife, died shortly after giving birth to a baby girl, but before she passed away, she asked my grandmother to raise her child and take care of her husband. And she did—this was just the kind of person my grandmother was.

In my memory, my grandmother is a little old lady, with short gray hair, hunched from years of hard labor. She dressed in only the most minimal attire, and you could tell by the wear on her face that she'd had a rough life. Still, you'd never have known it by the way she acted and talked—she was elegant, and she never once complained about raising five children plus grandchildren. In this regard, my grandfather was little help. To be honest, I don't remember him being around all that much, and when I did see him, he was completely contained, always holding himself away from the family, a presence in the background. He and I never got close.

This was not the case with my grandmother, whom I adored. She ran a grocery store out of the front of our house. Because just about everyone in my neighborhood was as poor as we were, she sold soy sauce by the tablespoon and rice by the cupful. She was there minding the store all day every day, and many days I'd hang around. While she was attending customers, I'd help out by cutting open bulk bags of rice or fetching items from the back as she directed me in her commanding yet gentle tone. I looked up to my grandmother—her life hadn't been easy, but she'd worked with what she had and made her own way. I think I inherited the entrepreneurial gene from her.

My dad, on the other hand, was not the entrepreneurial sort, though he was a hard worker. Before and after his eight-year mandatory military service, he worked long hours chopping up logs, loading the firewood into a cart, and cycling all over town to drop it off at the homes of his customers. He didn't mind it; in fact, I'm pretty sure he preferred manual labor to any other kind of work. He wasn't interested in expanding his business beyond himself and just a few employees, whom he treated well and who respected him in return. I don't have many other memories of my dad from my early childhood because he was gone so much during the war. My grandma and mom were the ones who tucked me in at night and woke me up in the morning, who dressed me and fed me. They were also the ones who showed me what it meant to be a good person.

My mom worked as a teacher at a private school and also as a tutor. When I was little and still a good boy, she'd take me to school with her every day. After school, she tutored students at our house. While she taught, I did my homework, absorbing, I think, some of her skill and love for teaching. She was well known for her no-nonsense style and for keeping kids in line, which won her the respect of many parents in the neighborhood. She had to be strict—back then, there were fifty kids to a class, so everything had to be in perfect order or all hell would break loose. The teachers weren't shy about giving out spankings, and if that didn't do the trick, they'd take a ruler to your palm. If that still didn't inspire the student to shape up, they'd hit the back of the hand, where the skin was the thinnest. That hurt a lot, as I can tell you from experience. My mom didn't hesitate to get out the ruler, which came in handy when dealing with me once I started skipping school. In those early days, though, I only got into a little bit of trouble now and then, but it was the kind of trouble that every kid gets into before he or she knows better. Nothing that any kid exploring the world wouldn't do. Then, everything changed.

***

On paper, the Vietnam War (which, in Vietnam, we called the American War or the Resistance War Against America) ended in 1975, on the humid April day that Saigon fell. For most Americans, I think the Vietnam War calls to mind the social climate of the sixties and early seventies in America: the anti-war protests and the hippies and the draft dodgers and the young soldiers coming home with PTSD. In fact, the conflict had been going on in Vietnam for thirty years by then, its roots in the French colonization of Vietnam in the nineteenth century and the Japanese occupation after World War II.

Many Americans have heard of Ho Chi Minh—he was the guy who fronted the resistance against both French and Japanese rule. In the fifties, he led an uprising that ultimately led to the North-South division, with his communist party, Viet Minh, taking charge of the north, and anti-communist Ngo Dinh Diem taking over as president of the government of the Republic of Vietnam in the south. Around that time, the Cold War was heating up, and the United States decided to back South Vietnam because North Vietnam was an ally of the Soviet Union. It escalated from there—you've probably seen the movies or real-life photos of napalm bombs falling from B-52 bombers onto villages, of soldiers clearing the jungle with blowtorches and carrying their fallen comrades on stretchers through the grass, of helicopters spraying Agent Orange to poison fields and people.

By April 30, 1975, American soldiers had long been slinking out of the country with their tails between their legs, in a process Nixon called "Vietnamization," leaving us to fend for ourselves. I was seven years old and so didn't really understand any of this at the time, though it did affect me and my family. By the time Saigon fell, more than three million people had been killed, half of whom were Vietnamese civilians. While others were climbing the walls to the American embassy in a final attempt to get a seat on one of the helicopters evacuating the city, I was riding on the back of my uncle's motorbike. We hadn't heard from my dad in a long time, and we didn't know whether he was alive or dead. Like most able-bodied men, he had been in the military for the previous eight years, working with the allied US troops.

Anyone who had anything to do with the Americans or the South Vietnamese Army was fleeing or trying to hide. The government had already evacuated or dispersed, and the US ambassadors and those who could buy their way out had left in helicopters and overloaded airplanes that flew in bursts over the city. All was in chaos. People were looting abandoned shops and rioting in the streets, and men were stripping off their military uniforms and leaving the precious cloth on the ground where it fell—they'd rather be naked than shot. As the North Vietnamese—organized as the Viet Cong, a guerrilla network of communist agents and subversives, supplied and controlled by North Vietnam but active within South Vietnam—made headway into the South where I lived, those who'd opposed them were now considered the enemy.

I was at my uncle's girlfriend's house when the gunfire began. I hid under the stairs, listening to the sound of helicopter blades chopping the sky above and the machine guns with their rhythmic *dadadadadada*. Every so often, I'd hear the earthshaking thump of a helicopter crashing into a house nearby. I wanted my mom and my grandma. I would have even settled for my sister and cousins. But they were far away, back at home and probably hiding under the stairs too. The city went on lockdown, with everyone forced to stay inside for days. I don't remember how long it was, but the time that I was apart from my mother and grandmother felt like a century.

The war officially ended that April day. South Vietnam's president Nguyễn Văn Thiệu resigned, and General Duong Van Minh surrendered. The National Liberation Front raised its flag over the presidential palace. Saigon became Ho Chi Minh City.

Finally, after almost a year, my dad came back. He'd been captured, held as a prisoner of war, incarcerated, starved, perhaps beaten or tortured—I still, to this day, don't know the details. I was just a kid, and this was not something we talked much about. I knew only that the war was over and he had been released.

We'd had little hope that he'd ever come back, so when he walked in the door, we could hardly believe our eyes. The muscles he'd developed during his many years chopping and delivering wood had turned to skin and bones. With his hollowed-out cheeks and straw-like hair, I hardly recognized him. Despite appearances, my dad was incredibly lucky—when it came to labor or "reeducation" camps, the sentence and the actual time spent incarcerated often differed. People stayed in the camps for years and years, or disappeared entirely.

"I got shot in the leg," he told us his first night home over the usual meal of rice and vegetables. My grandmother had made sure to ladle out an extra helping of sauce for him. "Left leg, in the back and out the front. That stopped my running pretty quick."

My mother looked at me, then looked back at him and raised an eyebrow. "Maybe not fit for young ears?" she said.

"Nhuan, I think they've seen plenty. What does talk about a little leg wound matter? Anyway, it's better now. For a while there, I was afraid that they were going to have to amputate. There was hardly any food, let alone medicine or anything like that. Every night, I took a strip of cloth and pulled it through and threaded my leg like you thread a needle, then poured salt in to kill off the infection. Hurt like hell, but here I am, both legs intact." That kind of casual attitude was typical of my dad, and watching the way he dealt with life's struggles was probably how I formed my own laid-back attitude. Bad things happen; you survive. What's the big deal?

Still, the ways in which our world had changed had a big impact on us. The communists had taken over, "unifying" the country as the Socialist Republic of Vietnam. They kept everyone on a tight leash. Though technically free now, my dad was a designated enemy of the state. This was a label that was hard, if not impossible, to shake, and it would follow not just him, but his entire family. It meant that we always had to be vigilant—any word or action could be used against us.

It felt, to some degree, like all of us were prisoners of war in Ho Chi Minh City. A representative from every family was required to attend "reeducation" meetings twice a week, or else. Usually this was my mom or aunt or one of my uncles, who'd always return from these sessions exhausted and silent. I don't know the specifics, since I was too young to go or hear about it afterward, but I know attempted brainwashing was involved. Capitalism, the individual, Nguyễn Văn Thiệu, and the United

States were bad; communism, the collective, and Ho Chi Minh were good. According to the communists, the North had rescued the South from the oppression of the Americans. In reality, our lives became hell after the communists took over.

They considered people who were educated, like my mom, or even marginally financially secure to be guilty by default, because any success could be credited to corruption by the Americans or the evils of capitalism. We hadn't been wealthy before by any means, but at least we'd been allowed to run my grandmother's grocery business. We had always struggled to make ends meet, but under the new communist regime, things we hadn't considered to be extras we now had to skim back on.

We learned firsthand that the rejection of capitalism is one thing in theory but another in practice—and it makes earning a living really difficult. The new government looked for any opportunity to co-opt capitalist ventures. For us, that meant that all of a sudden, we owed many years' worth of back taxes on my grandmother's store, which we couldn't begin to afford. It was blackmail, a way to suppress the middle class and take control of everything. If you could pay, they'd let you keep your business open and relieve you of half your profits indefinitely. If you couldn't pay that big lump sum, well then, you had to shut down. My grandmother had to close the doors to her shop. Businesses all over the country closed, and more and more people went hungry. The police or desperation often forced healthy young adults to leave their homes to do farmwork in the countryside. A cloud of disappointment and helplessness hung over the city.

Because my family no longer had direct access to rice, seasoning salt, and other essentials through our store, we had to go out and buy from another grocer. My grandmother, instead of running her own operation, used her newly freed hours to go to the market to buy vegetables and a few grams' worth of meat to feed the entire family. The sauce we kids had always fought over became even thinner. Our bellies were always half-empty.

The co-opting of business wasn't the only way the new government worked to keep us poor and continually off-balance. With all the economic turmoil due to collectivization, inflation went crazy. On top of that, the communists would sporadically change the currency. I still remember one late evening, when the chairman made an announcement on all media channels: "Do not believe the rumors. We are *not* going to change the currency. No one should panic." The next morning, at around five o'clock, he made another announcement: "A new curfew will be implemented starting immediately. And there is going to be a change in the currency." Each household could only exchange a small amount, so the cash stashed under the bed or in the back of a closet suddenly became worthless, good only for stoking a fire or insulating a wall.

No wonder people didn't trust anyone. No wonder people lost faith in the future.

All of this meant many things, most of which a boy of eight wouldn't be able to grasp, at least not consciously. But I'm pretty sure that this was when I changed, when I went from being a decently behaved little boy to a little demon. Vietnam had become a more ruthless, dog-eat-dog kind of world, and I was a survivor.

Now, on top of trying to keep me fed and clothed, my parents and grandparents had to keep me out of trouble. This proved to be as difficult a struggle as everything else in our new life. Of course, I kept running off to gamble and get into fights and steal the neighbors' chickens, and I'd gotten good at hiding my crimes. Meanwhile, my grandmother had seemingly developed eyes in the back of her head, and she kept thin, foot-long sticks around the house so that she could grab one and give me a good whack. Back then in Vietnam, corporal punishment was the norm, not the exception, even for kids far better behaved than I—and, believe me, most of the time I deserved whatever she dished out. She was softhearted and had tried positive reinforcement, but it didn't get her anywhere with me. I teased my little sister, Kitty, and messed with my cousins Liem and Banh on a daily, if not hourly, basis. My grandma would say, "If you go for a whole day without making your sister or cousins cry, I'll give you some money." Rarely was I able to earn that reward—bullying them was an impulse I just couldn't resist.

Unlike my grandma, who could hit me only once before I'd make an escape, my dad always succeeded in landing multiple slaps and punches. One day, when I should've been eating dinner at home with my family, I had chosen to play marbles with friends instead. We were out in an alley by my house, and I was just about to take my turn—I had my sights on a friend's red-and-gold marble—when, all of a sudden, I felt a sharp pain on my butt. I cursed and turned around, ready to throw a punch—until I saw who had hit me: my dad. I don't remember what my punishment was for this particular infraction, but I do know that it was earned. I usually got the standard punishments, like having to go without dinner. Sometimes, especially as I got older, my parents would lock me out of the house for the night. (Although my grandmother, kind soul that she was, would usually sneak me in after they'd gone to bed.) Other times, if I'd been really bad or had aggravated my dad too many times in a row, I'd get a beating. When my dad punished me, he did damage—often it took me weeks to heal.

For every assault on his misbehaving son, there were a hundred ways in which my dad sacrificed for the family. There was always food on the table, even if the meals consisted mostly of rice, with some veggies and sauce on top. As happened in so many families around the world, even those who had plenty of food, we kids always battled over who would get the biggest helping, especially when it came down to the sauce. We'd look forward to every second and sixteenth of the lunar month, when people worshipped the god of prosperity and wealth in business, usually by offering a whole chicken. It wasn't because we were particularly religious that these days were so eagerly anticipated; it was because on those two days of the month we had meat. Believe me, after days of rice and vegetables, chicken—even a small piece—looked incredibly tasty. But my dad always waited until everyone else had been served before he took his turn.

"When do *you* eat?" my grandma would ask him.

"Let the kids eat," he'd reply. Though I have no doubt that this was a selfless act, my dad might have also had an ulterior motive. In our poor neighborhood, those who liked to drink usually had to make a financial choice: buy food or buy booze. If you chose the latter, you got the bonus of getting drunk faster on an empty stomach. Often after dinner, my dad would go find a few friends in the neighborhood and drink cheap alcohol, usually white wine or beer. I never saw him act belligerently, though. Usually, he'd get a little tipsy, but he always seemed in control.

My dad's carousing inspired one of my first entrepreneurial endeavors. By the time I was about twelve or so, I'd discovered a lucrative business opportunity within the adult ritual of evening drinking: selling peanuts. I'd buy salted peanuts in bulk, then divide them among a bunch of small plastic bags. This was before vacuum seals or anything like that, so I'd light a candle, fold over the plastic, and heat it up to make a seal. At the earliest opportunity after dinner, I'd sneak away from the house with the peanuts and run off into the night. Then I'd walk through the streets, selling these baggies to folks out drinking on the sidewalk. Salted peanuts weren't as decadent as chicken wings, barbecued ribs, fried cheese sticks, or any of the food that drunk North Americans like, but I always sold out.

It quickly became apparent to me that running a business—meeting people, making money—was much more exciting than reading books or sitting in class listening to some uptight teacher drone on and on. Like seemingly every adult on the planet, my teachers were always looking for reasons to punish me. And even if they didn't have a good reason, my family was Chinese, and that was reason enough. My dad had been born in China *and* he'd been in the South Vietnamese Army, so he had two strikes against him. Even though my mom had been born in Vietnam, the fact that her parents were Chinese placed her side of the family in an ethnic minority as well. This made me an outsider. The kids made fun of me for it, but I didn't take it lying down. I got in lots of fights, and I was punished often.

When I was nine or ten, I had the great honor of being beaten by the principal himself. In accordance with my usual recess activity, I'd been fighting and running around the classroom and generally inciting a riot. Jumping up and down on a chair by an open window in a second-floor classroom, I accidentally elbowed a potted plant. It fell through the window and hit the ground below in an explosion of soil and ceramic shards. A little girl had been playing nearby—had it landed a few inches to the left, it could've killed her.

My so-called friends didn't hesitate to betray me. I was sitting quietly at my desk, the expression on my face nothing less than angelic, when the principal opened the classroom door and walked in. He and the teacher exchanged a few whispers.

I pretended to be really focused on the papers on my desk. My teacher scowled.

"Hao," she shouted, "get up here." In front of the entire class, he had me lie facedown on the teacher's desk. The fact that the principal had taken time out of his busy schedule to come to our classroom to discipline me was a big deal. He rolled up his sleeves unhurriedly, then took hold of a stick he'd brought especially for this purpose. I could hear the sound of sweaty palms squeezing, like he was making sure his grip was strong enough to deliver maximum impact. The room was absolutely silent, and I could feel fifty pairs of eyes on me and the target—my butt.

Whack! I didn't move. Whack! Whack! I held my breath. A minute passed. I had made no sound, but in my mind, I was calling the principal every bad name I could think of.

"OK, Hao, you may return to your seat," my teacher said. I stood up and calmly walked down the aisle between the desks, determined not to show any reaction. My butt hurt like hell.

Did that beating teach me a lesson? Of course not. Out of necessity, I had become hardened to the world. I couldn't escape the facts: I was a Chinese minority, my dad had been in the military, my mom was educated. All of these were strikes against my family and me, and there was nothing I could do about it. They—the other students, my teachers, anyone in a position of authority—were going to pick on me no matter what, so I'd adapted by being one step ahead, picking the fight first. I refused to learn anything from these kinds of experiences, though in that particular instance, I couldn't sit for a week afterward. A good kid respects authority, a bad kid doesn't, and I'd become a bad kid. It was as simple as that. I wasn't mad or resentful or even ashamed—I didn't feel a thing.

CHAPTER 2

Dreams of Escape

Before Saigon fell, the schools had a curriculum that would've been fairly recognizable to a Westerner. But after the communists took over, the books and lessons were filled with communist propaganda, which my parents were not happy about. The teachers even encouraged the students to spy on their own parents! If we reported any suspicious activity or conversation, we'd be greatly rewarded. They'd usually fail to mention the terrible punishment our parents would receive. Because of this and my never-ending antics, my mom stopped trying to force me to go to school. Still, she was determined to give me an education no matter how much I resisted and, knowing that her disobedient preteen would never let her tutor him herself, she hired a math tutor and a Chinese language tutor. I'm sure she worked out some kind of friends-and-family discount within her tutoring community; otherwise, I have no idea how she could have afforded it.

From the beginning, I was good at math. Not so much at reading Chinese, though I loved *wuxia*, Chinese Kung Fu novels. Based on Chinese history, these books have been popular among the Chinese for many generations. *Romance of the Three Kingdoms*, *The Legend of the Condor Heroes*, and *Two Peerless Heroes* were some of my favorites. I idolized those heroes—they were incredibly wise, and they had superpowers acquired through lifelong martial arts practice. Using these powers, they fought evil and protected the weak.

Since we had electricity only five days a week and rarely in the evenings, I'd spend most nights reading these books by the oily yellow light of a kerosene lantern. In my mind, I was the star of every action sequence, incredibly powerful but so very humble. Much too humble to show off my powers, of course, or reveal that I could kill an enemy with barely more than a blink of an eye. I stayed up late with those books, dreaming of being a superhero, of being powerful and in control.

Other nights, I'd gather with friends outside a neighbor's house to watch TV—the only legal television on the street. It belonged to a government agent who was allowed such a luxury. Kids and adults would crowd nightly around his living room window, peering through the glass to watch an episode of some show, produced in Vietnam and screened by the government. These shows were usually tame with some kind of uplifting or unifying message appropriate for the good communists we were supposed to be. The only show I can remember with clarity is an old opera—not exactly what a young boy wanted to watch. Still, this entertainment was better than nothing, a distraction from the colorless world the communists had forced us into. Whoever came the earliest got the best view, and the man kindly left the door open so that we could hear the program, though we had to look through the grated metal security gate to see the grainy black-and-white screen.

Since Western movies were banned, a black market had developed around TVs, tapes, and VHS players from Hong Kong. Some nights, a group of us would gather behind closed doors to watch whatever bootlegged film was available on someone's black market TV. Usually it was a Bruce Lee and Jackie Chan movie, from early in their careers. Our watching these movies was a big deal—we'd be in huge trouble if we got caught. When I was about twelve or thirteen, some of my Kung Fu fantasies actually started to come to life when I began practicing martial arts. Initially, I was drawn to Kung Fu because I believed it would improve my bullying effectiveness and efficiency. I already considered myself an expert in beating up my sister and cousins, but I, so dedicated to self-improvement, wanted to work on my technique for neighborhood fights. My mom supported me, though for other reasons. She thought it might help me to let off steam, and so she again dipped into her tutoring income to pay for my lessons.

Now, four or five times a week, I'd get up at five thirty in the morning so that I could go to practice in the park at dawn, to run drills on the hard-packed red mud, sweating under the rising sun. Barefoot and wearing only thin black pants, I learned discipline of body and mind under the tutelage of Kung Fu master Sifu Li. He was an unassuming man, short, with a round face and chubby body. You'd never have guessed by looking at him how powerful he was, or that he had been a high-ranking officer in the Viet Cong. Rumor had it that he'd come south to fill some high executive position—we knew enough not to ask for details. But whenever one of his students got arrested, the master simply would walk into the jail and exchange a few words with the guards, and that would be that. He saved many a young person from the reeducation camps.

Despite my bad intentions, I eventually realized that you learn martial arts not to be a better bully, but to develop the ability to protect yourself and those around you. My Kung Fu "brothers" and "sisters," as we called one another, were a good influence, particularly Quan, a senior practitioner. In the evenings, he and I would ride our bikes over to Sifu's house, a twenty- or thirty-minute ride through town over a bridge. Sifu wanted to train us to follow in his footsteps in Traditional Chinese Medicine, so he attempted to teach us meridians, herbs, diagnoses, that sort of thing. We'd sit in the living room, and he'd pull out a thick book and go through it page by page, reading aloud and pointing to charts and diagrams. I pretended to understand, but really it went right over my head. I kept pretending for a long time because I wanted Sifu to like me, and I enjoyed the company. I waited patiently for the moments when he'd close the book and teach a vital Kung Fu move, like how to knock someone out. I learned a lot from Sifu, and a lot about him. He'd been a pro fighter, and he was a good man. He taught me not to bully, but to focus on self-defense and protection only. Sifu really helped me get my head on straight. Well, in some ways—at least he helped me to channel some of that macho aggression into a disciplined practice and not take it out on my sister and cousins, just as my mom had hoped. My Kung Fu dreams began to take on a realistic form, though it still involved my defending the innocent through bravery and feats of strength: I decided I wanted to be a police officer when I grew up.

After a year of studying under Sifu, I no longer got into fights or bullied, but of course there were plenty of other ways I could get up to no good. I listened to Sifu's authority, but I was still rebellious at home, self-centered, and defiantly independent. And I still had no interest in my math or Chinese lessons.

My mom knew that I'd be better off somewhere else, somewhere that had opportunities for a teenage boy with a lot of energy to make the best of himself, somewhere that didn't have military service that was mandatory for all boys. She was careful not to show her beliefs, however, at least not in public. The communist regime's eyes and ears were everywhere, and we had to be mindful at all times of our speech and behavior. Any hint of discontent was grounds for jail, the seizure of property, or worse.

So, if my mom couldn't get me to go to school, and if she couldn't get me out of the country, then she needed to find something to occupy my time so I wouldn't spend all day getting into trouble. A trade, something that would keep me off the streets, teach me responsibility, maybe even get me to help pay the bills—that was what I needed. She knew that the opportunity to earn money was one thing that could convince me to sign on. First, I tried an apprenticeship with a mechanic. That didn't work out—I wanted to drive the car, not work on it. Then my mom set me up to apprentice with a jeweler, and right off the bat, I discovered I had a knack for it.

Master jeweler Kong rented a room above a store near our home, located on a busy street. He was tall and skinny, with a noticeable hunch earned from so many hours stooping over his work. He chain-smoked all day, every day, lighting one cigarette with the last embers of the other. I inhaled his smoke as he stood behind me, teaching me how to use my tools, how to melt down a gold ring and turn it into something else. Back then, we used a foot pump to stoke the flame. You'd give it a pump, and fire would shoot out the end. I thought that was pretty cool.

Not only was my mentor a master jeweler; he was also a master drinker. He dressed nicely, with his shirt always tucked in, but he always smelled like alcohol, even when he wasn't drunk. Customers didn't seem to notice, or if they did, they didn't mind. He had a good reputation, and customers came in and out all day to sell their old jewelry, or get a ring resized, or see what he might have for sale.

He taught me many things, some of which my mom would have been less than thrilled about, had she known. From him I learned how to party, how to drink bad booze and smoke cigarettes. Soon I, too, was smoking more than a pack a day—the cheap, filterless, pre-rolled kind that made an unaccustomed throat raw. You got used to it, too, building up some kind of throat callus, and then they'd be the only thing that would do the trick. Every day we'd fill the small workshop with smoke, leaning over our wood desks, squinting through the magnifying lens and the smoke at the diamond ring or the necklace or whatever other jewelry we were holding in our nicotine-stained hands, a cigarette dangling out the side of each of our mouths.

After work, I'd go hang out with Kong at one of his friends' houses. Though the venue changed, the activity was always the same. We'd sit on the living room floor of whatever ramshackle house we'd come to that day and pass around a shot glass and a bottle of booze. When every last drop had been drunk, whoever's turn it was would then go out to get more, and we'd repeat the cycle until we were all completely wasted. Now, remember, this was the cheap stuff, firewater that left you with one of those nails-through-the-skull headaches come morning. It was a completely different experience from drinking a good bottle of wine, believe me.

Sure enough, if we didn't have the money for some decent alcohol that might spare us those terrible hangovers, we certainly did not have enough money to spend on food—and we did get hungry. Sometimes one of us would go out and buy peanuts, the kind I'd sold when I was a kid just a few years earlier. Other times, we got creative.

Like this one time, when the Dragon, Tiger, and Phoenix Feast came to be. Fancy name, right? Sounds like something you might find on a menu in an upscale Chinese restaurant. Well, it wasn't as nice as it sounds: the main ingredients were dog, cat, and rooster. These animals just happened to be in the wrong place at the wrong time—the cat on a nearby roof, the skinny stray dog in the alley, the rooster at a grocer down the street. Throw them together in a huge pot, with some herbs and whatever else was around, and we had ourselves a tasty meal.

For the record, dog meat is delicious. And, in case you're wondering, as a kid I did have a pet dog, whom I'd loved dearly before he was hit by a motorcycle and died in my arms. Still, I enjoyed a little dog meat every now and then. I wouldn't eat it today, but if you think about it, it's really no different from a cow or a pig, which most Americans have no qualms about eating. Rumor has it that pigs are smarter than dogs, anyway. Not that I loved eating all little furry animals: I couldn't get myself to eat cat, in part because I didn't like the taste and smell and in part because I'd heard somewhere that doing so would bring bad luck. So, for you cat lovers, you can be comforted by the fact that I picked the greasy chunks of cat meat out of my bowl and gave them to a friend.

After all that, still drunk as a skunk, I'd get on my bike, and, in later years, my motorbike, to head home. I do not recommend drinking and driving—I could've been killed or gotten someone else killed. I was a complete and total idiot. Somehow, I always managed to swerve my way toward home, stopping every now and then by the side of the road to throw up. At home, I'd fall off my bike in front of my house, stumble to the door, and wake up the whole neighborhood by pounding on it. Then I'd take a deep breath and hold it, stepping back a couple feet from the door so that when my mom opened it, she wouldn't be able to smell the booze on my breath. I'm sure she knew exactly what was going on—she was and is no dummy, unlike her son. But she was always too tired to question me, so she'd just open the door and go back to bed. Immediately, I'd go inside, hug the toilet, throw up until there was nothing left in my stomach, and pass out.

No surprise—the next day my head would hurt so bad that I wished I could chop it off and be done with it. As you might have guessed, my commitment to those 5:30 a.m. Kung Fu practices had started to wane. And I wasn't sticking to a tutoring schedule, either.

As soon as the headache went away, I forgot about it and the behavior that caused it. That evening, I'd start all over again. It was pure stupidity. But hey, we've all been young once, right? Still, it feels like a miracle I survived all that. Ultimately, my own physical limitations saved me. My master and his friend thought drinking was the only way to live, and to be honest, I couldn't keep up with them. On top of that, I was learning a lot but wasn't yet making real money. Patience is required to learn a skill, and patience was not something I had, so I started to look for other ways to spend my time, other ways to make a fast buck.

Did I mention that this whole time, I'd been trying to escape Vietnam? Many families were trying to get out, and parents went to great lengths to smuggle their children out in the hopes that they could find a better life. Just as the war had been background noise before the fall of Saigon, the years afterward were a strange limbo in which I was living my daily life—ditching school, going to Kung Fu, getting into trouble, learning how to set a diamond—and trying, with my family's help, to escape. In fact, I'd tried to escape at least ten times since 1975. So far, nothing had worked out; there were tons of ways for an attempted escape to fail. In some instances, the arrangements would turn out to be a scam, a grifter taking my family's money and promising a way out of Vietnam without having any real plans to follow through. When that happened—and it happened more than once—there was nothing to be done but admit defeat and start saving again for the next try. More often, the timing would just be off in one way or another: The boat would come too soon or too late, or the bus would get a flat on the way to the beach. Sometimes we'd hear a noise or see a light and think the police had discovered us, and we'd scatter like a bunch of scared seagulls, sand flying as each person ran in a different direction.

Every time was a big gamble—but you only had to hit the jackpot once. At first, my goodbyes with my family were heart-rending. Hugging wasn't part of our culture, but to show their affection, my mom and grandma would give me a red envelope with a little cash inside, for good luck. I had mixed feelings: On the one hand, I was scared, afraid that I might never see my family again or that I might die. On the other hand, I was excited to be running toward freedom. And for me, excitement proved more powerful than fear.

Eventually, these efforts became so commonplace that I didn't think about them much in my day-to-day life, and at a certain point, my family and I no longer had the difficult goodbyes we shared at the beginning. Instead, we'd have a last meal celebration, and then we'd say goodbye almost casually, like I was going off to run an errand or to go for a walk around the block, each of us trying not to think about the dangers ahead.

When I turned sixteen, I decided that I'd had enough. I was tired of using my energy on what felt like an impossibility, tired of seeing my family's efforts and money go to waste. I stopped tutoring in full, and I stopped my Kung Fu lessons. I decided to focus my efforts, instead, on making a life in District 1—specifically, on becoming a big shot, a big fish in this tiny pond. I wanted to make money and impress girls and hang out with my friends—what else does a teenage boy need, after all?

So, I started my own welding business with my mom's cousin, whom I called Uncle Quoc. I bought virgin metal and turned it into screws, bike sprockets, clothes hangers, and other easily assembled and necessary items. Someone had told me, "With girls, one rev of a motorcycle's engine is better than a hundred sweet words." So, with the money I earned, I bought a motorcycle and rode the busy streets of Ho Chi Minh City, very much feeling like the big shot I was trying to be as the engine growled beneath me. Now and again, I'd stop by to see the jewelry master and his friends and inevitably drink myself stupid. Often, instead of returning home to my disappointed but resigned mother, I'd sleep on a mat in the Buddhist temple nearby, too drunk to be bothered by the hard tile floor or to feel shame about passing out in a sacred place.

This relatively carefree life lasted two years, until I turned eighteen. I was happy, and in a certain sense free—free of responsibility, and free to make money and spend it how I pleased, as long as I kept it all under the radar. I had cash in my pocket, and I was feeling good—young and invincible and doing what I wanted, when I wanted. With all that going on, what was tomorrow to me? The very idea of a future had receded even more into some unexamined place in the back of my mind. And then, the local authorities knocked on the door.

I wasn't home on the morning, just after my eighteenth birthday, when the two government officials arrived. The first thing my dad did after greeting them at the door was to hand them some cigarettes.

"My son is working at the moment," he said. "He hardly comes home anymore."

"Yes, well, as you know, it is time for him to do his duty for our country. It is time for him to go into the military," said the shorter of the two.

My dad was very well liked in the community, and he'd been bribing these two gentlemen, among others, on a regular basis. That was just how the system worked. The stakes had been raised, and so now he'd just have to bribe them some more.

"Next time you see your son, have him report to the station."

"I sure will," my dad said, slipping them some bills to buy me some time.

Though the Sino-Vietnamese War had technically ended in 1979, China and Vietnam were still fighting over their shared border. The war had different names based on whose side you were on. The Vietnamese called the Sino-Vietnamese War the War against Chinese Expansionism, whereas the Chinese called it the Defensive Counterattack Against Vietnam. Because my family identified itself as Chinese, I felt that by being in the Vietnamese army, I'd be forced to fight my own people. I'd have to serve—maybe even fight or die—for the communist oppressor.

I wasn't willing to do that. So, it was time to try to escape again.

CHAPTER 3

Too Close

It was an hour or two before dusk, the time when the heat of the day started to lift. The fees had been paid, and I walked with Linh, a neighbor girl, to the prearranged meeting place to catch the bus. Our moms were family friends, and they'd decided that we should go together.

Linh and I took our time on the walk, keeping our voices low yet casual as we talked about what we thought the West was like. We had no idea of the reality—to us, it was a fantasy, a place where all our dreams would come true. Were someone to see us, they'd think nothing of it, assuming we were just two neighborhood kids out for a stroll. At least, that was what we hoped they would think.

At first, everything went smoothly. A few minutes after the bus dropped us off, a motorcycle pulled up, and we both got on the back. The driver took us to an amusement park, called Suoi Lo Ho, out in the countryside. We were told to walk around like we were just a couple of kids having a good time. I could hear the music and the noise of games being played farther into the park, the sounds of crank trains and cars, and people joyfully screaming. I smelled dough frying and meat cooking. Children meandered by, licking ice-cream cones.

We'd been told to stick to the front of the park, near the entrance, so I never did get a chance to go back and ride the merry-go-round or see the souvenir shops and games for myself. We saw some other people wandering around near the front, too, and we suspected that they were going on the same journey as we were. I felt very conspicuous.

After an hour or so, a truck arrived and stood idling outside the gate. Someone gave us the cue, and we and the other loiterers left the park. I was quick and light, and I jumped into the truck without effort. But Linh had a harder time getting up, and she got lost in the crowd of people scrambling to get in. Just before the truck was about to leave, I caught sight of her and grabbed her hand, helping her in.

A military-style canvas sheltered the truck bed, and it was totally dark inside, with standing room only, our bodies pressed up against one another. The air was humid with the moisture of our sweat. Though I'd been through all this before, I was nervous—the stakes were higher this time, and the repercussions would be more serious now that I was nearing adulthood. I was full of youthful bravado, but the stories of the prisons and the labor camps were sobering. It wasn't uncommon for someone to just disappear. No one talked openly about attempting to escape, but usually we'd find out later during hushed backdoor conversations that something had gone wrong and so-and-so had gotten caught. Rumors would fly, tales of brainwashing and forced labor and all kinds of other horrors. When—if—people returned, they were usually greatly changed, hardened from manual labor, haggard and grizzled from long hours sweating in the fields, sometimes maimed or silenced by the torture that was too horrible to talk about. Sometimes their families, too, were punished, sent to camps or forced out of their homes to become farmers for the government. Many people didn't come back at all.

The truck started with a hiss, and the dull murmur of the passengers quieted. I patted Linh's hand and gave her a brief smile. She looked queasy, her skin taking on a greenish tinge.

"Stick your face up to the cracks of the tent," I said. "The air will feel nice."

The truck trundled along, rattling through neighborhoods with simple buildings, two or three apartments stacked high, their balconies open to the street. Children ran along the sidewalks, shouting, while their mothers called them in for dinner. Young men and women carrying canvas bags walked briskly, and older people with weathered faces plodded along. The sights and smells were so familiar to me that I hardly noticed them. Instead, I focused on the truck's rumbling, willing it to go faster toward our destination.

After what felt like years, the truck pulled over and stopped with a groan. We were silent—there was no luggage to be gathered, since, in case we were caught, we didn't want to appear as though we were going on some kind of journey. With a politeness not often seen in the city, each of us waited our turn to jump off the truck and make our way toward a cottage alongside a river.

I stepped off the truck to find that the air had cooled a few degrees and dusk had set in. I didn't know where we were, exactly. I could feel the soft dirt underfoot, and the smell of sediment, water-logged vegetation, and decaying fish guts filled my nostrils. The Saigon River flowed lazily by and, by some miracle, an old thirty-foot fishing boat was sitting in the water just offshore.

Still no headlights. No sounds of gravel under tires, no shouts to halt, no sound of rifles being cocked. This was good, as good as we could hope for.

A big crowd was already sitting on the floor of the cottage when we entered—we weren't the only group to have paid for this trip. As usual, the captain had agreed to take on more passengers than was safe. Of course, more passengers meant more money. And the risk he was taking on was great, perhaps a one-shot gamble and therefore worth every extra penny. We sat down and joined the other group, and then came the waiting. After thirty minutes, I heard someone say that all males should go out first, through the back of the house. I followed the other boys and men, giving Linh what I hoped was a reassuring nod before stepping outside. The group headed to the river.

"Get in and wade out there," the same person said, pointing to the boat standing fifty feet away. Quietly we walked out, water filling our shoes and mud tugging at our feet, then climbed up into the boat.

"Steady now," whispered the captain, whose high cheekbones and surprisingly smooth face I could just make out by the last light of the setting sun as he extended his hand to each of us in turn. "Shh, quiet, don't rock the boat."

The girls and women arrived one by one and boarded, pushing those who'd come earlier to the sides and back of the boat, until we were all standing, squeezed together like cigarettes in a pack. *When will the captain consider this boat full?* I wondered. There was probably room for fifty or sixty people, and I guessed that we were getting close to one hundred. Luckily, Linh managed to find me in the crowd. "I'm sure we'll be leaving shortly," I said to her.

Finally, when it would have been absolutely impossible for one more person to get on, the captain reeled in the anchor and pulled the engine's cord. It came to life with a smoky cough, and I held my breath as he maneuvered us out into the river. After a few minutes of chugging along with the current, we picked up speed. There was a collective sigh of relief.

The next few hours were uneventful. Darkness had fallen, and those of us crushed to the inside of the boat lifted our faces toward the sky to catch a breeze and a glimpse at the stars. I'd done this before, so I knew what those on the edge were seeing—the city passing by, the lights of houses and businesses still open, the dark, unoccupied land along the shore. I could hear the faint chirping of crickets, the sound of the wind and the boat engine, and every now and then, I'd pick up a smell of dinner cooking, of charred meat or fish stew. Linh stood beside me, the cotton of her shirt brushing against my arm every now and again. I was comforted by her presence, someone familiar next to me as we moved toward the unknown.

All of a sudden, the boat stopped, throwing us forward as one.

"Goddammit," the captain swore. He pushed people aside, making a beeline for the side of the boat. We watched him lean over one edge, then make his way to the other side, where he did the same. He returned to the helm, where he switched the gears back and forth between forward and reverse, just like you'd do to try to get a car out of the mud. No movement—just the sound of grinding.

"Hey, you," he said, pointing to a group of young men huddled next to him. "You know how to swim?" They stared at him, their expressions blank. "Who else?" The captain looked around. "Anyone who can swim, go on, get out and push." One by one, people dropped over the side of the boat. I took off my shoes and joined them, the water reaching to our waists. Together we surrounded the boat, staying clear of the propeller's sharp blades under the water. For a solid half hour, the captain shout-whispered, "One, two, three, push!" while we strained against the boat.

Nothing happened. Well, something did happen, but not what we were hoping for—we caught the attention of three river patrol boats. They approached us, and an officer on one of them took out his gun and fired a shot at the sky.

"We know you're trying to escape!" he yelled. "Nobody move. If you run, you'll get shot!"

Without a moment's hesitation, Linh and I took off and ran toward the shore, along with a majority of the others. I could hear the *dadadadada* of a machine gun behind me, and I swear I could see sparks as bullets whizzed by. The mud slurped at my bare feet, and the weight of the water pushed against me, slowing me down like I was in a bad dream. I didn't dare stop—if I was going to die, I'd rather die running.

Suddenly, I noticed that Linh was no longer by my side. I turned around and saw her farther out in the water, stumbling and splashing. "Go!" she yelled as I made my way back to her. "I'll only slow you down." We both knew that if only she, as a young woman, were caught, the sentence would be much lighter. If we were caught together, my punishment would likely be much worse. Still, what kind of guy would leave his companion behind? Back then, I was agile and long like a monkey, and I reached her quickly, grabbed her arm, and began to drag her to the shore. "Come on," I said. "We came here together; we're getting out of here together."

A cluster of palm trees blocked our way, so we kept running along the beach, our arms and legs pumping. My heart felt like it was about to explode from fear and maximum effort. Of course, speedboats were faster than two running teenagers, and soon one caught up, just passing us and stopping at the shoreline ahead.

"Linh!" I grabbed her arm and stopped her, nearly yanking off her arm from the halt in momentum. "Don't move."

We froze. I could feel beads of sweat gathering across my forehead. I held my breath, hoping that would somehow make me invisible. The beam of a flashlight swept across the water; the river looked like a wall, impenetrable in the night. The light circled out toward the shore, exposing colorless dirt and colorless stones and colorless grass. I could just barely feel Linh holding her breath beside me. The light swept side to side, coming closer. I could feel my heartbeat in my chest, my throat, my face. Fifty feet, forty feet, thirty feet. Pause. Twenty feet. Pause. The light passed over both of our bodies, but for some reason, the harbor patrol failed to notice us. Time froze, but my heart kept going, racing inside the stillness of my body. I prayed that they couldn't hear it.

The light pulled away with the sound of the boat moving forward in the water. We both gasped for air. And then, we ran.

For a while, we went as fast as we could, eventually finding an opening in the trees and making our way in from the shore. As the adrenaline began to wear off, we slowed to a walk, finally able to get a sense of our surroundings. The ground was now dry and hard-packed. The lights of a neighborhood loomed ahead.

"What should we do?" Linh asked. I looked around, unsure.

"We have to find someone who can help us," I said. By my guess, it was probably close to midnight, too late for it to be reasonable to go knocking on doors. But we had to get home—if the police knocked on *our* doors in the morning and our parents couldn't account for our whereabouts, the police might be able to link us to this escape attempt. At that very moment, they were probably already surrounding the city, rounding up anyone out past curfew. If they caught us, they'd punish our families and haul us away. I wasn't going to let that happen.

"C'mon," I said. "Let's go this way." We walked farther into the neighborhood. Being far outside the city, it was mostly quiet, with only a few houses scattered in the darkness. At the first door, we came to, we stopped. I rapped on it with my knuckles, and after a few moments, I could hear footsteps.

The door opened a crack.

"Who are you?" a middle-aged man asked, glaring at us through his rimless glasses.

"We need a ride home. Can you help us?"

He looked us up and down—no doubt he could tell immediately what we'd been up to. Our feet were caked in dirt, our pants and the bottoms of our shirts soaked. His face softened. At this point, we had nothing to lose, so I told him everything. He seemed pretty nice, and it was too late not to lay all the cards on the table. "We need you to take us on a boat to catch the ferry. Will you?" If he said no or threatened to turn us in, my plan B was to beat him senseless. (This was always my plan B—except for those times when it was my plan A.)

The man held out his hand, palm up.

Linh and I glanced at each other. She shrugged. Then I remembered my ring, a heavy gold one I'd bought after my motorcycle. I'd purchased it because I liked the way it flashed in the sunlight, sure that it caught people's eye as I rode by. I pulled it off and placed it in this stranger's palm.

"Here," I said.

He held it up and looked it over, then put it between his teeth and bit down.

"It's real," I said. "That's an ounce of gold right there."

The man examined the ring for teeth marks and, not finding any, put it in his pocket. "OK," he said. "I have a boat. I'll take you to the ferry. But you'll have to wait here for a few hours." He opened the door wider, and we stepped inside. The kitchen was small but clean, with a round table and three chairs, and a stack of dishes drying by the sink. "Sit," he said. "We'll leave at first light."

Linh and I sat down heavily, and the man left us there. After a moment, I heard a door close and some whispering. The house fell quiet, and all we could do was sit there and hope that he wouldn't turn us in, or that the police, who were certainly combing the area, wouldn't knock on the door.

It was still dark when the man came out of his room and gestured for us to follow him. Silently, we left the house and walked back toward the river. Our footsteps were quiet, absorbed by the dirt beneath us, which was beginning to soften as we neared the shore. His boat was one among many others along the shore. He untied it, tossed the rope in the prow, and pushed it out toward the water. Once it was floating in the shallows, we got in. Linh and I took a seat in the back, happy to let this stranger drive.

If anyone stops us, I thought, *we're screwed.*

Thankfully, no one did. As a red sun washed over the city, we caught up with the ferry. The man paid our fare, and the captain let us climb aboard.

It was still early morning by the time we got home. Linh and I parted ways at the corner near my house, and she walked on toward her own house, where my future wife was likely sleeping.

"Oh my," my mom said when she opened the door. "Get inside." I stepped through the doorway, my legs feeling like they were about to give out from under me. "Where are your shoes? You're filthy. Are you hurt?"

"No, Mom, I'm fine, really. Just tired."

I passed the day half-asleep. My sister and cousins hadn't been too surprised to see me, and my grandmother acknowledged my failed attempt with a pat on the back. "There's always next time," she said.

That evening, after dinner, I dragged myself up to my sleeping area at the top of the stairs. I was so tired, I could barely keep my eyes open as I began to undress, ready to take a much-needed shower before finally surrendering to sleep. I moved my hand toward my heart to check its beat; then, suddenly, I was wide-awake—in the armpit of my jacket, a few short inches from my heart, was a bullet hole. *Oh shoot!* I thought. *A bullet hole. A bullet hole!* Then I laughed. *How lucky I am to be alive!*

CHAPTER 4

Captured

An essential part of the survival game under the communists' rule was acting casual at all times. Of course, we were content with our lives! Of course, we were *not* planning to escape! Why would we? Everything was great! So, for the next few months, it was business as usual: welding, riding my motorcycle, making money, and being young.

My dad had continued to bribe the local authorities in order to delay my military recruitment. But that was only a temporary solution. Eventually, I'd have to go—if I stayed in Vietnam.

So, my family was still very motivated to get me out. A few months later, my mom found another escape opportunity.

"Hao," she said one evening over a dinner of rice and water spinach, "next week you're going to catch a boat."

It was a protocol similar to the previous time, and all the times before. I, along with a few dozen other people, caught a bus in Ho Chi Minh City and rode southwest for forty-five miles to MỹTho City, located in the Mekong River delta. Arriving at dusk, we were more than a little surprised to find a big-bellied fishing boat waiting for us and that things were, for once, going according to plan.

This time, though, the boat looked newer, and the crowd smaller. There were only seventy or eighty people, and we fit on the boat with much more breathing room than on the previous vessel. As the sun sank low in the sky, we began our slow journey along the river toward the South China Sea, the water gradually changing from deep blue to sepia to black. Along the way, we passed houses on stilts with rusted tin roofs, small fishing boats docked below them. No one waved.

Finally, we reached the harbor. In the dark, I could barely make out the inspection station up ahead; it was just a black silhouette against the black night. The captain pushed the bottom-heavy vessel to full speed, then cut the engine, the boat gliding forward on its own momentum. As a group, we held our breaths. In the darkness and silence, every minute felt like ten minutes, a year, a decade. I couldn't see any movement at the inspection station, and the captain's steering seemed steady and calm. *Maybe we've made it past*, I thought.

Then a flare lit up the sky, its pink light reflecting off the black water. *Oh shit. We're in trouble now.*

The captain turned on the engine and hit the gas once again. If we could just make it to international waters, we'd be safe. Suddenly, the boat's big belly felt like, well, a big belly. No way could we outrun the scrappy little patrol boats, but we were going to try. It was too late to turn back.

Two patrol boats caught up to us. "Stop, or we'll shoot!" a man yelled, his voice amplified through a bullhorn. Our boat kept going, its course not changing an inch. I could see the outline of the captain, his shadowed face looking forward, unmoving. Then came the bang of a gunshot and the sound of a bullet meeting the wood of the hull. The captain, and everyone else, hit the deck. Lying on his belly, propped up on one elbow, he continued to steer the boat with one hand, his extended arm in grave peril. Another bullet, and another, hit the side of the boat and landed on the deck.

Please, Buddha, I prayed as a bullet whizzed by, directly over my head. *Please.* All around me, I could hear the whispered prayers of the other passengers to all their various gods. I didn't care whose god was in charge, as long as someone saved us. To this day, I have no idea how the captain continued to steer, but somehow he managed, and we kept going into the night, darkness on all sides except for the patrol boats' lights.

This went on for an hour, then another, the patrol boats right behind us like a couple of dogs nipping at our heels. Suddenly, a loud crash in the water rocked the boat. A grenade? I wasn't sure. But whatever it was had missed us, so we kept going, full steam ahead. Babies were howling, children were crying, mothers were shushing. A few minutes later came another crash, this time closer than before. I could feel the vibration of it through the planks pressed to my chest. Still, the boat was unharmed, and we kept going. Ten minutes later, a third warhead hit, this time connecting with the boat on the port side. One of the cabin's windows shattered. A child screamed.

"Stop!" a woman yelled. "Captain! Stop! My son!"

It was chaos on the deck. A young boy, maybe ten years old, had been hit, and even in the dark, you could see the dark stain spreading across the back of his white shirt. "Captain! Please! My son, my son is hurt. We have to stop!"

The captain turned off the engine and rushed over to us to get lost among the passengers. If the patrol officers identified him as the one in charge, his punishment would be execution by gunshot on the spot. The boat slowed, then stopped, and the patrol boats pulled up on either side. Six soldiers hopped aboard.

"You know," one of them said, all cavalier as he took over the wheel, "we were all out of bullets."

"Yeah," said another, "and that was our last bomb. If only you'd kept going . . ." The other soldiers laughed. To this day, I don't know if they were telling the truth, or if they were just messing with us. I prefer to think the latter—otherwise, it's too much to bear.

It was dawn by the time we made it back to the harbor. The little boy had stopped crying, and his mother was gently rocking him in her arms, murmuring softly. As the sun emerged from the water, light poured in through the bullet holes in the sides of the deck. We pulled up to the dock, and two of the soldiers climbed out and tied up the boat.

"Who's the captain here?" the soldier who'd piloted the boat asked. We all looked at one another, looked at our feet, looked at the sky, said nothing.

"I said, who's the captain here?"

Still nothing.

The soldier patted his pistol but didn't take it out. "Tell me, who is the captain?"

"I think he jumped in the water," an old man said.

"Yeah, I saw him jump," said a younger man.

"Oh, he jumped? Well, how lucky for him. Tie them up," the soldier said, waving his hand dismissively.

The soldiers came around, one by one, and tied each person's thumbs together behind their backs. We shuffled single file off the boat and onto the dock, where they tied us together in a line. This was how we had to walk, along the pier and then through the city. I felt like everyone was staring at us, though I'm sure the people on the streets looked away, not daring to acknowledge this procession in hopes of avoiding the same fate. I kept my head down, utterly humiliated.

Finally, we were loaded into the police trucks and hauled off to jail.

***

"I'm sixteen, sir."

"What year were you born?"

"The year of the dog, sir."

He punched me in the face. I was so thirsty, and the blood in my mouth tasted of iron and salt. I didn't know if it was day or night, and I couldn't remember how many times I'd been pulled out of my cell for questioning. I had no idea how many times or hours I'd been there. Each time, I lied through my teeth, determined to keep my real age a secret. I had destroyed the only evidence of my age, my birth certificate, which I'd torn into a million pieces and thrown into the river. I tried to make myself look younger, which mostly meant that I pulled out my leg hair when the guards weren't looking. What else could I do? Adults— those over eighteen years of age—would face two years of "rehabilitation" in a labor camp for the crime of attempted escape. By law, minors could only be held for two months. Of course, actual jail time didn't always match the sentence.

The officer hit me again, this time with the back of his hand. "How old are you?"

"Sixteen, sir."

"What year were you born?"

"The year of the dog, sir."

Another punch to the face. And so on, for hours, for one day, two days, the same questions, the same answers, the punches and slaps and kicks, the hunger and the thirst. I didn't fight back, just as I'd been taught in my martial arts training. Instead, I tried to go with the flow, letting the force of the abuse ripple through me. They didn't let me sleep for more than an hour or two at a time. At the end of what I was pretty sure was the third day, the officer started in again.

"How old are you?"

"Sixteen, sir."

"What year were you born?"

"The year of the dog, sir." The kick to my stomach took my breath away, sending me and my chair against the wall as a unit. We slammed hard against it, and then sank to the dirty concrete floor. I gasped like a fish out of water. The guard leaned over me, sideways in my vision.

If I ever see you in Ho Chi Minh City, I'm going to kill you, I thought.

And so began my fifty-nine-day incarceration.

***

I was transferred from the temporary jail to a prison, where one hundred fifty men shared a single cell. It was a long, rectangular cement block, roughly the length of two shipping containers end to end, with a twenty-five-foot ceiling and windows way up high that let in just a little light. That was mostly OK by me, as the grimy walls and dirty men were the only sights to see.

Quickly, I learned the informal seniority system, in which the newcomers were shoved to the back by the stinky toilets. The stench there was unbelievable. Slowly, if you were there for long enough, newer prisoners would take your place, and you'd make your way up toward the front, where the air was fresher. A fellow prisoner, whom everyone called "the Director," seemed to be in charge of this system. He was a lifer, and therefore had had plenty of time to establish his authority among the other prisoners and make connections with the guards and the outside world. I never did learn the nature of his crime, or that of the crimes of anyone else, for that matter. We were all thrown in together—the escapees, the enemies of the state, the burglars and rapists and murderers—and because of the small space, we all slept on our sides in rows, like spoons.

I spent the first couple weeks of my imprisonment in the back, trying not to inhale the foul smell too deeply. I really cannot describe how bad it smelled, and it didn't matter that I lived with that smell twenty-four hours a day—you never, ever got used to it. There was nothing to do to pass the time, so for all those days, I simply sat there in the heat, sweating and trying to breathe through my mouth and counting the seconds until dinner, and then the seconds until bedtime. Sometimes, I curled up in a little ball and took a nap. With so many men crammed into the cell, there was not even enough room to pace, though often during the day, some would clear out to do mandatory labor, so I could stretch a little.

During those long initial days, I dreamed of the scent of flowers or the sight of a pretty girl or the sensation of swimming in the cool waters of a river. I yearned for one of my Kung Fu books to read or my guitar to fiddle with or a soccer ball to bop around. Anything to help pass the hours. Only twice a day was there something to do: eat. This went fast, because the prison fare wasn't good and the servings were small, especially for a growing boy such as myself. A bowl of plain broth and a scoop of plain rice—that was it. Water, too, was in short supply. Every three days, we received a bucketful, which I tried to ration as much as possible. Every sip left the taste of tin in my mouth and hardly put a dent in my thirst. I had this fantasy of ice water—a big, full glass of it, filled to the brim with ice, the condensation around the outside of the glass cold in my hand. I'd lick my dry lips with my dry tongue, imagining that first sip, the cool water sliding down my throat, spreading through my body vein by vein. As my hunger grew, I fantasized about biting into a succulent chicken drumstick, the skin crispy and salty, and about the feeling of tearing the meat off the bone with my teeth.

Besides napping and eating, the only thing to do was to talk to my fellow convicts. For the most part, people were friendly— you'd never suspect that the man you were shooting the breeze with was a cold-blooded killer. We talked about everything but also nothing, especially *not* the topic of what brought us to the prison. And certainly not how we felt about it. Many of the inmates had much longer sentences than I did, and their incarceration had become their new normal. There was no point in talking about the past or a future that would likely look exactly the same as the present. I didn't mention how much I was looking forward to leaving, or that every day felt like a year. That would have been impolite.

On day ten, my dad showed up. Having had his own prison experience, he knew how the system worked, so he'd brought cash—some for me and some for the guards. I didn't get to see him, but the guards, their pockets freshly lined my family's scraped-together funds, told me he'd been there. He knew that

I would give a false year of birth, because that was what we'd planned to do in case I were caught, and so he had no problem verifying my birthday when checking in.

After he left, I used the money that had made it to me to bribe the Director. I knew that my family must have made some kind of crazy sacrifice in order to get me that cash. I tried not to think too hard about whether this was going to mean less food on the table for Kitty and my cousins.

From day one, I'd been using what today some of my colleagues might call my "networking skills" to get in with the Director and his buddies. I knew that if anyone could improve my lot, they'd be the ones to do it. Even though I was a small-time delinquent and whatever they'd done had been bad enough to get them put away for life, we became pals. In addition to money, my dad had brought pork floss that I could heap on the daily scoop of plain rice, and salted instant noodles, which I could put in my plain soup and watch expand. These additions gave flavor and substance to otherwise bland meals, and, to be honest, after those first couple weeks of intense hunger, I actually ate better in prison than I did on the outside. I didn't have to steal the neighbors' chickens or hunt a stray dog to do it, either.

As they say, food is the way to a man's heart. This certainly held true in prison, where food was scarce and hearts were hard. Knowing this on some level, I shared my pork floss and dry noodles freely with the Director and company, and because of that, I was soon able to move farther away from the latrines and that stomach-turning smell.

They also say that money talks—in my experience that's most definitely true, no matter where you are. I was happy to place my funds in the well-oiled machine of the Director's bribery system. I gave him money, and, after taking a cut, he would give it to the guards. They took their healthy cuts of it, too. Then, when they felt like it, they would get me food. The wife of one of the guards happened to be an excellent cook, and sometimes she would prepare a home-cooked meal for me, some grilled chicken or caramelized pork belly, in addition to the fresh sheep's milk she brought a few times a week. I noticed a shift in the way I understood the world, my life, my parents . . . something like perspective. Hunger followed by fullness can do that to a person, even a little punk like me.

Besides managing the bribery pipeline, my new buddy the Director was responsible for job assignments. Every day, the head of the camp would give work descriptions to the Director, and if the jobs were hard, say carrying mud or moving bags of sand, he wouldn't assign me. If, however, they were light, like washing tiles or pulling weeds, he'd put me on the list.

The first day that I was allowed out of the cell, I cried. After so many sunless, stuffy days, the first breath of fresh air was like a rebirth. I tipped my face toward the sun and closed my eyes, feeling—really, feeling—its life-giving warmth as if for the first time. And, for perhaps the first time in my life, I felt truly, deeply grateful.

On occasion, we'd be assigned work cleaning streets or doing construction on government sites in the city. During the ride in the horse trailer with the other prisoners, I'd peer through the windows, watching the familiar busyness of My Tho City passing by. I knew that, by law, I should be released within sixty days of imprisonment—if, that is, they didn't discover that I wasn't actually a minor. *What if they never let me out?* I'd wondered as I watched the city pass by outside. In that case, I'd have to find a way to escape. The other prisoners and I would often talk about it while we hammered nails or shoveled dirt in the afternoon heat. *There are only two guards on duty,* we'd muse. *We could all run in different directions so they wouldn't be able to catch all of us.* We never actually tried it, though—our zebra-striped uniforms were just a tad too conspicuous.

The sight of a girl walking by would abruptly end our conversations. We were a bunch of men who rarely saw anyone besides our own dirty, ugly selves, and I was a teenage boy, after all. Even if she was on the other side of the field or down the road, we'd stop and stare, slack-jawed. I missed girls. I missed my life—my friends, my motorcycle, my business, my freedom. My family.

I had plenty of time to think, in particular, about my family, to mull over my past and the bad things I'd done. I thought about my future, about what I would do differently when—if—I got out of prison. For the first time, I was experiencing isolation, helplessness, frustration, fear, and regret. This was all very strange for me—I'd never really had these kinds of feelings before. I realized that no one truly cared about me except my family. I missed them—my grandmother steaming vegetables in the evening, my mother grading papers at the kitchen table, my sister telling me about her day. They'd given me everything they could, working extra hours to pay for my tutoring and my Kung Fu classes and my escape attempts, and I'd taken them for granted. What kind of son doesn't appreciate his family? I'd been ignorant and selfish. How could I have treated them that way? I swore to myself that when—if—I got out, I would never take them for granted again. I would appreciate my life. I would be a good son and a good person.

***

Day fifty-five. Fifty-six. Fifty-seven, fifty-eight. And then, finally, day fifty-nine. I'd been keeping close track of the days in my mind. One more day and I would at least know if they were going to keep me past the two-month mark. By then, I wasn't exactly hopeful about being released. There was just too much outside of my control, too much left to chance. Maybe they'd figured out my real age and just hadn't gotten around to telling me yet. Maybe someone had claimed I'd expressed anti-communist sentiments in exchange for leniency. I'd survived this long, so I knew I could keep on surviving, but the not knowing had made the days feel longer, the cell more crowded, the soup more tasteless.

That fifty-ninth evening, I was sitting in the cell as usual, chatting and sweating and generally killing time while waiting for dinner. Then the cell door opened. A man wearing a green prison-guard uniform and hat stepped in. "Lam Vi Hao," he called out, "you are going home." I was stunned, unable to move from my seat on the floor. The other prisoners, however, were visibly thrilled. Whenever anyone was released, the whole cell got really excited. "Go on!" a cellmate said. "Get a move on!" Someone clasped my shoulder and gave it a shake. "You're going home!"

I blinked, shook myself, and stood up. The others knew that I would not be allowed to take anything with me, so they gathered around as I pulled my little bag down from the ledge where I'd stored it. "Here," I said as I handed out my food stash, a little bit to as many people as possible. "Here you go." I was so excited that I gave away my money, too. I was going to be free! Who needed money when you had freedom?

There was no time for heartfelt farewells, not that anyone would've been interested, anyway. "Bye!" I called over my shoulder as I walked out the door, knowing that, with luck, I would not see any of them again. (In fact, many of them are probably still there, growing gray and stooped, and maybe having no idea how the country has changed in the last twenty-five years.) I walked out of the cell with nothing but the clothes on my back, signed some paperwork, and that was that. I was free.

Well, it didn't take long for me to realize that freedom is much, much better with money. It was a twenty-minute bike ride to the bus station, and a two- or three-hour bus ride from Mỹ Tho to Ho Chi Minh City. Out on the street, I looked around at the traffic, the people walking by, everyone going about their normal lives. It was busy and familiar, the noise and exhaust a comfort to me. I didn't spend too much time taking it all in—I was antsy to get home.

I tried to hire a cyclo, one of those bicycle rickshaws in which the passenger sits in the front. But as soon as the drivers discovered I was penniless, they took off! "Please," I said to one after the other, "I need to get to the bus station so that I can get home." Three or four of them stopped long enough to tell me to go to hell before swerving away. Given the location and my grimy appearance, people might have suspected that I'd just been let out of prison, so some of them were likely afraid that I was being monitored and that they might get into trouble for helping me. More than that, they couldn't spare the time and money. I mean, how often do you stop to give change to beggars on the street?

Then, thankfully, a cyclo stopped. "Poor kid," the driver said. "I'll take you." It was a Sunday, a beautiful, clear-skied afternoon that was especially, indescribably, beautiful to me.

I climbed in. "Thank you, sir."

He said nothing, just pulled into the stream of traffic. I swear, the air that flowed past us had never been sweeter. I was going to savor all twenty minutes of it. But I was worried about figuring out the next leg of the journey.

A few minutes later, we pulled up next to a young woman on a bike, just as the line of traffic came to a halt. She was tall and thin, and well dressed.

"Excuse me, miss?" I said gently, so as not to startle her. "I just got released from jail." I saw the surprise on her face. "I'm not a bad guy," I said quickly. "The reason I was in jail was that I tried to escape the country. Now I just want to go home to Ho Chi Minh City, but I have no money."

She looked at me for a minute, and I could see kindness in her eyes. "OK," she finally said. "I'll give you the money." She and the cyclo driver pulled over, and the woman gave me a wad of cash, more than enough to get me home. I wanted to cry with gratitude, but I didn't. Instead, I asked for her address.

"I'll pay you back," I said.

"No, don't worry about it."

"No, really, I insist."

"OK," she said, shrugging and probably thinking, *Yeah, right.* She took out a pen and a scrap of paper from her purse and wrote down her address.

"Thank you," I said, taking it from her.

That woman was an angel. I think about her all the time— what kind of person would do that? Would you have given a young man just out of jail your money? I wouldn't have. I couldn't comprehend her kindness; I didn't deserve her kindness. This type of thing never happened in my neighborhood. I had been a scammer, not a philanthropist, always taking whatever I could, never giving. I was surprised by her generosity, and the generosity of the cyclo driver. He'd given me a free ride. Why did they do that for me? *Wow,* I thought as I headed toward the bus station across the road. *There are kind people on Earth.*

Nowadays, if I see someone with a sign saying they need money for bus fare, I remember that woman and give them some cash. I have a stack of dollar bills in my car for that purpose, and my wife likes to give cereal and energy bars, too. When my kids were young, I had them hand out the bills. I told my boys that these people might be drug addicts, but it didn't matter. We didn't know their situation, and they were very unfortunate. We had a home and they didn't, so we should share a small portion of our good luck.

At the bus station, I bought a ticket and, from a food cart near the terminal, a plate of rice with a pork chop. I ate quickly, sitting on a bench and keeping an eye on the road. Mothers holding their children's hands passed by, men with worried expressions paced or stood still, gazing off into the distance. The bus, which was one of those converted military ambulances with a canvas roof, arrived shortly, and I followed the line of people aboard, taking a seat on a bench. Soon the bus was filled to capacity with fifteen or so other people. I had a good three-hour ride, with many stops along the way, to think about recent events, my good luck, and the kindness of strangers.

I walked home from the bus station in Ho Chi Minh City. It was the dry season, the air crisp. I relished the sight of every familiar landmark, taking in the cyclists riding by, the women hanging laundry from balconies above, kids running and shouting just as I had done a few years before. The light breeze cooled my skin, and I ran a hand through my hair to do what little I could to make myself presentable.

"Daddy! Hao is home!" my mother yelled after opening the door. She grabbed my hands and held them tight, smiling broadly. My dad and my grandmother and Kitty and the cousins gathered.

"Are you all right, Son?" my dad asked. My sister and cousins started right in with questions about prison. What did I eat? Where did I sleep? Did I make any friends?

All I could do was nod. I felt their love, really felt it, in a way I never had before.

"Leave Hao be," my mom said after a minute. "Can't you see how tired he is? Come, I'll make you something to eat."

Just then, my exhaustion hit me, and I practically stumbled through the door.

"But first, go shower," my dad said. "Then eat."

The rest of the day passed like a dream. I showered, luxuriating in the clean water. I ate, really tasting my mom's home cooking. I was elated and tired and grateful—going from jail to home was like going from hell to heaven. Soon I fell into my bed; it had never felt softer.

***

The next day, I did the dishes for the very first time in my life. This simple act astonished my entire family. It astonished me too. That's hard to believe, I know, but it's true. Before that, I'd never done anything for my family, not a single thing. But jail had changed me. I wanted to be a better person now. That terrible time was worth the life lesson. I'd had fifty-nine days to be completely powerless, useless, helpless. I'd had fifty-nine days of being treated as less than a human being. I'd had fifty-nine days to reflect on the kind of person I wanted to become.

And now I had a chance—a chance I hadn't been sure I'd ever get—to put it into action. Back at the metal-recycling company that I ran with Uncle Quoc, I treated my employees with a new-found friendliness and respect. I was nice (or, at least, nicer than I had been) to my little sister and cousins. I said please and thank you once in a while. I still rode my motorcycle, but with a little more humility than before. I felt fortunate to be alive, and to be free.

CHAPTER 5

One More Chance

A couple months later, in March of 1988, my parents told me that they'd arranged another trip. This time I'd be going with Lisa, Linh's sister. I didn't know Lisa all that well, but our moms went to the same Buddhist temple and we were family friends, even though they lived a couple blocks away in a nicer neighborhood.

Lisa and I were opposite in just about every way—where I was an uneducated street kid, she was elegant and delicate and incredibly smart. Where I avoided academics at all costs, she'd gone to a French school, and besides Vietnamese and Chinese, she knew English and French. We did have one thing in common, though: she'd tried to escape, too, and failed, along with her sister, Shirley, a friend named Yen, and a cousin. She'd even made it all the way out to international waters, but the boat's engine had failed, and a terrible storm had nearly capsized the boat, broken engine and all. By some miracle, a nearby ship had spotted them and kept a spotlight shining on the boat throughout the night, and when the storm had passed, they'd sent a small boat out to meet them. The envoy gave them two options: they'd tow the boat of stranded escapees back to Vietnam, or give them food and water and then leave them behind. Since the engine didn't work, what that really meant was either you come with us, or we leave you here to die.

The people on the boat begged the rescuers to tow them to a nearby country that accepted refugees. But the ship was from communist East Germany—this was before the fall of the Berlin Wall—and its allegiance was to communist Vietnam, not to those trying to escape it.

And so, they reluctantly picked the first option. Back on shore, the group was immediately hustled off to jail. Packed in with the other women and children, Shirley developed a dangerously high fever. The guards took her to the hospital, but the next day she returned. "I saw a ghost," she said, and, terrified, had chosen to forfeit rest in a hospital bed in order to be with her family on the hard-packed dirt floor. Her temperature continued to rise, and the guards took her back to the hospital. As soon as her fever broke, she cried and begged to be taken back to the cell. Once returned, she got sick again.

After all this back-and-forth, the guards released Lisa and Shirley. I'm not sure whether this was because there were too many people in the cell, or because they had a sliver of compassion left for women and children, or simply because they were tired of dealing with them. Whatever the reason, Lisa might not have been accompanying me on this trip had she stayed. Yen, after giving multiple bribes, finally got out of jail six months later; Lisa's cousin, a young man over eighteen, spent nearly two years in jail.

***

The night before our escape, Lisa's mother decided to keep Shirley behind. Their mother, probably thinking about the previous attempt, had been too worried to eat or sleep. Maybe she was having a hard time seeing the reward beneath the shadow the risk cast: Even if both daughters managed to escape, she wouldn't see them for who knew how long. If they didn't, or were lost at sea, or kidnapped . . . for any mother, that loss is too terrible to imagine. At any rate, only Lisa met me at the bus.

Once aboard the bus, I placed the bag of crackers beside me and unwrapped the plate of rice and pork chop my mom had packed for me. Since getting out of jail, I savored her home cooking in a new way, and this time was no different. My mom had packed this food for me, and I felt that new feeling of gratitude as I took the first bite.

Suddenly I realized that it was my birthday—in the commotion of getting ready to escape, I'd forgotten. I was twenty years old, though according to the state, I was only seventeen. Tears came to my eyes. There I was, on my birthday, trying to escape instead of celebrating with friends and family. I felt so lonely and sad, and for a moment my mind went blank, too overwhelmed to consider the thought that I might never see them again, and that this could be my last birthday.

For eight hours, the bus rolled along in the falling dusk, lulling its passengers into something like calmness, each of us occupied by our own thoughts. I had plenty of time to think about where I had been and where I was going. Would I make it to freedom? If I did, would I be worthy of it? These kinds of questions ran circles in my mind, and I realized that I was finally starting to understand the concept of "tomorrow."

Sometime in the middle of the night, the bus came to a stop. I couldn't see anything in the pitch black, but I could hear the sound of water flowing by. We had arrived at Nha Trang, where we were supposed to board a boat. We were ushered into a house to hide and wait. Off and on we slept, not knowing when the call would come to leave.

Early the next morning, we were told to get back on the bus, which pulled out with a screech and returned to the road. To this day, I have no idea what happened—one of the lookouts posted there must have seen something and signaled danger, so it was back to the starting point for us. For another eight hours, we bumped along in the direction from which we'd come, our stomachs cramping with disappointment and our legs and backs cramping from so much sitting.

After a total of sixteen hours on that bus, I was happy to breathe in the comparatively fresh air of evening in Ho Chi Minh City. Lisa and I walked to her house, and her mom made us dinner. We didn't talk much—what was there to say?

Just as I'd swallowed the last bite of rice, there was a knock at the door. Lisa opened it to find a young man, our contact, on the doorstep.

"It's back on. Be back at the bus in ten minutes."

Another eight hours later, we were back in Nha Trang. By the time we got to the beach for the second time, it was around 2:00 a.m. The trip's organizer used a flashlight to signal toward the ocean. The moonless night stayed dark. He flashed the light again. Nothing. And again. Finally, after five or six attempts with seemingly endless waiting, a flash came in return, and I could just make out a small wooden fishing boat stealthily approaching two hundred feet from shore. The tide was low, and so the boat couldn't get very close—we'd have to meet it out in the water.

For half a second, we were silent, as though we were all holding our breath and weren't quite sure it was safe to let it out. Then, suddenly, we began to move fast, everyone panicking, pushing to get to the front and pouring out of the bus as fast as we could. Every minute, every second counted—the police could show up at any time, and if they did, we'd all be finished. If I got caught again, who knew how long I'd be in prison—maybe forever. Or maybe I'd be shot.

I tumbled out the bus door and onto the sand, then turned around to help unload four tanks of water. Another young man and I carried one of the tanks to the shore.

Two other buses had pulled up while we'd been waiting, and their passengers were also flooding out their doors. In a frenzy, we all ran toward the shore, our feet sinking into the sand, people falling and struggling back up, bags and packages and shoes left behind to form a strange trail from the now-abandoned buses to the water.

Someone shouted, "Whoever can swim go straight to the boat. Whoever cannot swim get into a fishing basket." Lisa and the other people alongside me hit the water at a sprint. The water was balmy, my clothing suddenly heavy after being submerged. People pushed one another and splashed through the water, and those who fell got stepped on as everyone desperately struggled to get ahead. The bag my mom had packed for me kept slipping around in front of me, getting in the way and slowing me down. *The fish will appreciate all the crackers,* I thought as I flung it away. The clothes on my back were now my only possessions, but there was no time to think about such things.

Two rope ladders had been thrown over the side of the boat, and soon it became apparent how athletic you had to be in order to climb up. I was young and fit, and I grabbed onto one of those ropes, holding tight to it because the side of the boat was very slippery. I shimmied up it like a monkey, and, once on deck, turned back to help pull other people up one by one. In the scuffle, I'd lost track of Lisa. I scanned the crowd in the water below. People were clambering into the boat, and, closer to shore, people were fighting for space on large bamboo baskets. Some of the baskets were becoming overcrowded and sinking, leaving people thrashing about in the water. Finally, I saw Lisa—she'd managed to get into a basket with three other people, and the basket was being pushed out toward the boat. How I could tell it was Lisa I don't remember—it was full dark, and the people were black silhouettes against the black night.

A moment later—when they had reached a halfway point between the boat and shore—a big wave came and flipped the basket, spilling Lisa and the others out into the ocean. I couldn't see anything beyond some splashing, but I'd find out later that she'd nearly drowned, not because she couldn't swim but because someone had grabbed onto her and wouldn't let go, pulling her down with him. She tried to swim up, but he held on with all his might, so she'd swallowed salt water into her lungs and choked. To free herself, Lisa had to bite the hand grasping her so that she could swim away and toward the boat.

"My wife," a man called out behind me, struggling to make his way along the crowded deck. "Has anyone seen my wife? She's seven months pregnant. Please, has anyone seen my wife?" Those who even bothered to acknowledge him shook their heads. After a few more minutes of searching, the man walked over to the side, swung his legs around so that he was sitting on the railing, and pushed himself off. His splash went unnoticed, but his motionless body floating up to the surface is something I'll never forget. He must have hit his head on the boat on the way down or on a rock hiding under the water. A few people loaded him into a basket, and some others pulled the attached rope to lift the basket up and onto the deck. Once we were out to sea, we discovered that his wife had never made it aboard. She'd been left behind in the water and was perhaps thinking that, at that very moment, he was on his way to freedom while she was turning back toward dry land. This kind of thing happened often enough—people would get separated and then reunite across an ocean or two. But that wouldn't happen for this couple—the husband never regained consciousness, and we buried him at sea the next day without ceremony.

A couple of months later, we learned that, after not hearing from him, the man's wife had desperately asked around for news of him. The organizer of the escape avoided her. The woman found out that Lisa had been on the boat, so she visited her family. Though they'd heard from Lisa that the woman's husband was dead, they dared not tell her the truth because they worried for her and her baby—she was about to give birth. I've always wondered: How did she eventually learn of his death? What did she tell her child about its missing father?

Lisa, meanwhile, had made it to the boat. She managed to find me in the crowd—I felt a tug on my arm and turned around. There she was, this tiny little thing, probably not even ninety pounds and soaking wet. Somehow, she'd gotten through all the people kicking and climbing and falling. She was soaking wet and nearly incoherent with exhaustion, but other than that, seemed to be all in one piece. As she'd neared the boat, someone had pushed her down or landed on top of her, and she went under. Later she told me that she could hear the motor and had been terrified that she'd be chopped up in the blades. "I almost died!" she said. She had managed to swim away from the crowd and find an open space to surface and catch her breath. Spotting a big boulder sticking out of the water, she swam to it and climbed up with her last ounce of strength. A few others had found this safe haven as well, and, as a group, sat still and quiet, watching the chaos surrounding the boat from afar. From that perspective, Lisa could see that it wasn't just one or two ropes dangling down; there were ropes all around the boat, but everyone had come from the same direction and had all tried to climb the same rope. Even as she saw that, she'd thought to herself, *Fine, I give up.* She was just too tired to go on.

Fortunately, the organizers found her and refused to accept that decision, helping her through the water to the boat. If they hadn't, she probably would've stayed on that rock, and the rest of this story would have unfolded in a very different way.

***

The boat was probably meant to carry only forty people max, and I'd guess that there were at least a hundred of us. I also knew from experience that that didn't necessarily mean more people wouldn't be coming. As we sat in the ocean, the boat rocking beneath us, I wondered if the boat might sink from our weight. I was anxious to leave, to get as far away from shore as possible. Why weren't we moving? Suddenly, the captain emerged from the cabin and onto the deck.

"Cuong?" he shouted, seemingly unaware of the volume of his voice. "Are you there?"

No response.

"Cuong?" The captain scanned the deck. "Has anyone seen my son? He's twelve years old, about this high," he said, holding his hand at chest level.

No response.

"Cuong? We can't leave until I find my son."

Silence. I shifted on my feet, feeling my cold wet jeans and T-shirt sticking to my skin and praying that the captain would find his son so that we could be on our way. The other passengers were looking around, peering over the edge of the boat, glancing at one another and shrugging.

"Cuong?"

"I'm here, Dad," a child's voice called out from the dark.

Reassured, the captain made his way back to the helm. The engine started, and we noisily took off.

Everyone pushed their way down into what was less of a cabin and more of a storage area. That way, if another boat were to pass by, they wouldn't be able to see the hundred-plus shivering people stuffed inside and, hopefully, they'd assume that our boat was just going on an everyday fishing trip. If someone did catch us at that point, they could do just about anything, the worst-case scenario being that they would rob us first and then bring us back to Vietnam. Rumor had it that this was what happened 90 percent of the time.

With all that extra weight, the boat chugged along laboriously, slowly, like it was dragging itself through the water by sheer will alone. Inside the storage area, there was no sitting room, no room to lie down; we were packed in like sardines. Soon it began to smell with all the smells that humans produce, especially when afraid and crammed together into a tight space. This also just happened to be where the gasoline was stored, and every breath I took was mostly fumes, making me feel more and more light-headed.

The next hours are somewhat hazy in my memory. In fact, I can't really recall much of that night—Lisa had to fill me in later.

She said that, after hours that felt like years, the night turned blue, then gray. As day dawned, the captain signaled that we'd cleared the coast guard and could come out. She and the other passengers filed out onto the deck, their bellies rumbling and their clothes still heavy with water. Lisa looked around and couldn't find me. She went back below into the storage area, and there she saw me, completely passed out in my soaked clothes. I'd been too close to the gasoline tanks, she guessed. She tried to wake me up but couldn't and asked someone to help drag me up onto the deck. It took a while, but finally they managed to wake me up.

With the sun up, illuminating a hundred tired faces, the captain determined that Cuong wasn't among us. I'll never know who impersonated the boy the night before, but whoever it was had helped more than a hundred people on their journey toward freedom. Thinking that he'd left his son behind in Vietnam, the captain was, understandably, furious. (A few weeks later, after we'd landed in the Philippines, that anger would be replaced by grief when someone finally revealed to him that they had seen Cuong's body floating in the water before we escaped. He had gotten stuck between the wood of the prow and the ladder and broken his neck. The captain wasn't the only bereaved parent— another boy had developed appendicitis and died upon arrival. This was a gamble, with very high stakes. And this time, many people lost.)

I'd never felt so sick in my life. My head ached something terrible, and I was shivering despite the heat. The sunlight in my eyes only made my headache worse, though it did help to dry my wet clothing. I'd been planning to take care of Lisa. That was why our parents had put us together, after all. I, as the boy, was supposed to keep her safe. But she ended up taking care of me. "It's OK," Lisa said over and over. "You're going to be OK."

Someone distributed the water from the metal tanks, giving each of us a single capful. It wasn't even enough to wet my lips. I felt like I had a layer of chalk in my throat, but we had to ration every drop because we really didn't know how long we would be out there under the boiling sun.

That first day, the ocean was calm. By the second day, my headache had thankfully disappeared. I remember vividly that first look around once I was able to sit up. On all sides was a vast silver ocean as far as I could see. Our boat was like a little grain of rice going somewhere, maybe nowhere, it didn't matter as long as it wasn't back to Vietnam. We only needed a compass to make sure we were going in the right direction, the direction away from home.

We had motored our way into international waters, where we'd be safe from the communists, but fair game for pirates. But I didn't even have the energy to worry about that possibility. All I could think about was how thirsty I was. We all were. People dipped towels or shirts in the ocean, then laid them on their faces or backs to cool off. I did the same, and every now and then, when the thirst got really bad, I'd touch my tongue to the cloth as though it wouldn't be as salty as it had been the last time. My ice-water fantasies from my time in prison returned full force, taking up a majority of my consciousness. As my chapped lips cracked and bled, I imagined a giant glass of ice water, clean and clear and cold, the condensation cooling my hot hands, the water washing away the chalk in my throat.

It didn't take long for me to regret throwing away my bag of crackers. Between us, Lisa and I had no food (Lisa had lost her bag when the bamboo basket flipped), but fortunately we'd become friends with a very kind young lady named Hang Tuong who'd brought tangerines and banh dauxanh, sweet little cakes made out of mung bean paste and sugar.

When she offered some to us, the friend she was traveling with said, "Don't give away your food! Are you crazy?" That was a reasonable question given the situation. A saner person might have saved her food in light of our unpredictable future, but Hang didn't listen to her friend. Quickly it became clear that she didn't much care about others' opinions. She was very pretty and looked strong, like some of the girls I'd known who practiced Kung Fu. Like someone who could hold her own.

Hang shared her food with us for the next few days. If I had been the one with food, I'm not sure I would have done the same. No words can express how much that meant to us.

Those little tangerines saved us, though we didn't always want food—there was plenty of seasickness and, as you probably know, when one person throws up, it's only a matter of time before a domino effect gets going. Bobbing along the expanse of the South China Sea minute after minute, hour after hour, with the bright sun in our eyes and the unknown ahead, we had plenty of reasons to feel sick. Because of the heat, we went back and forth between the storage area and the deck—the deck had air but was fully exposed to an unrelenting sun, while the cabin provided shelter but stank of gasoline and other unsavory odors. Remember, there was no bathroom aboard.

On the fourth day at sea, a miracle occurred: rain. I can't even begin to describe how happy we were when that first drop turned into a hundred, a thousand, a million. All of us stood out on the deck, our mouths wide open to the sky, the only sounds our swallowing and the pitter-patter of raindrops hitting wood. Those who'd brought raincoats held them out to catch the water. Some of the men took off their shirts and wrung them out, hoping that even without soap they'd be able to rinse at least some of the stink away. For that one day, we had enough to drink.

As darkness fell, though, the rain turned to a thunder-and-wind storm, and it felt like the whole ocean was shaking beneath us. The ride was so jerky, it seemed as though the waves had corners.

"Hurry!" the captain shouted at his helpers. "Tie these paddles to port and starboard. Quick now, before we capsize!" The raindrops came down sharply, like knives. Water spilled onto the deck and splashed from all sides. "What are you standing there for?" the captain yelled to the passengers. "You wanna get tossed overboard? Get down!"

We all pressed inside the storage area. The waves became as tall as mountains. The boat rode up and up and up the waves, then down with a crash, up and up and up, and crash. For the entire night, the captain stayed glued to the wheel, steering and resteering the boat to face into the waves as he fought against the wind and rain that seemed determined to flip us. I prayed to Buddha again and again as people around me passed out and threw up nothing from their empty stomachs, shouted, cried, and clung to one another. The floor became slick with bile and tears and sweat and rain and seawater. Minutes and hours passed, but I was too dizzy and sick to keep track. *Will we make it through the night?* I wondered. *Have I seen my last sunrise?* I missed my family, the sound of my friends' laughter, my house, and my trusty motorcycle. It was common knowledge that plenty of people disappeared on these trips, never to be seen again. Until now, I hadn't understood what that really meant. *We might not make it,* I thought, finally and fully comprehending. I wished I'd been a better son, a better brother and cousin, a better friend. *I don't want to die,* I thought. *I'm still young. I want to live. But I might not live. I might not live.*

The storm raged all night, the boat rolling up and down like a car on a roller coaster.

Suddenly, the darkness slipped away, and we entered a wormhole to another universe. The wind died, the rain stopped, the waves smoothed into glass. The boat stilled. We walked slowly, cautiously up to the deck. The light was a pale violet, and the air was fresh, almost sweet. People blinked, trying to take it in, and breathed long, deep breaths. All around us was calm.

Somehow, we hadn't moved, according to the captain. It was difficult to believe we were in the same position as the night before, riding the roller-coaster waves up and down, but never forward.

Relieved to have survived such a storm, we were not expecting anything beyond the pleasure of being alive. But then we saw a big ship, way off in the distance. We knew we were far from Vietnam and the Vietnamese coast guard, so all of us crowded onto the deck to watch. Slowly, the big ship approached our little boat and, still too far away for us to see its captain or crew, it circled us once, twice, three times. Then it stopped. We all looked at one another. "What is it doing?" we whispered to one another. The ship sat there in the water, still far, yet so close. Everyone was thinking the same thing: *Please. Please rescue us. Please give us food. Please give us water. Please show us the way to a friendly shore.* "Hey!" we yelled. "Hey, come here! Please!" We danced and waved our arms and jumped up and down and yelled and called to them for hours. They didn't respond, though surely they heard us. Whenever our boat tried to approach theirs, they backed away. We became desperate. "Please!" we shouted. "We're starving! We have no food, no water. Please, help us!"

After we'd spent a few hours circling the ship in desperation, it took off. Just like that, without warning and without making contact. "No!" we screamed. "No! Come back! Please!" A mass panic spread as we realized that it wasn't coming back, that the crew had decided not to rescue us, that they'd left us to die.

***

After the fall of Saigon, hundreds of thousands of South Vietnamese had fled the communist regime. At the beginning, the United Nations encouraged many countries to help out by sending rescue missions that would pick up boat people and either drop them off at a nearby refugee camp or take them back to their countries. But at the time of our escape in 1988, after thirteen years of mariners helping refugees, a new rule had been put into place: the country of any ship that rescued a boat became responsible for its passengers. So, many countries ordered their cargo ships not to rescue Vietnamese refugees anymore.

My aunt Lien, along with her husband and three-week-old infant, had experienced this firsthand. Back in 1979, their boat had been at sea for seven days when they first saw the shore of Malaysia. By this time, they'd managed to survive not one but two pirate robberies, which left the passengers and captain with nothing but the clothes on their backs and a single rusty knife. As harsh as that sounds, this was actually great luck—after all, no one was kidnapped to be sold into slavery or prostitution.

A boat, which might have been owned by the Malaysian government, approached. Thinking they were being rescued, the captain let the ship's sailors tie their boats together. But instead of pulling them toward shore, they began to tow them back out to sea. Lien's boat had a small engine, and being weighed down by so many people, there was no way to resist. Sometimes these towing boats pulled so hard and carelessly that they caused the vessel to capsize. Luckily, someone managed to cut the rope with that one rusty knife before they got too far. The boat took off, leaving them at sea without food or fuel. They'd been so close, but instead of landing on the Malaysian shore, they only made it as far as a small and uninhabited island off the coast. The captain asked a few of the younger people to head back to Malaysia to find help, and so Lien's husband, along with some others, got back in the boat, leaving the rest of the group hungry and helpless. This small group did make it to shore, where they were greeted not with food or water, but with rifle butts. Regardless, the Malaysian government had to take responsibility for these refugees.

***

If that was the situation in 1979, you can imagine what it was like nine years later, in 1988. Vietnamese boat people had been flooding in for years and years at that point, and the world had grown tired of us. Perhaps the world has a finite supply of compassion. As that ship grew smaller and smaller on the horizon, our panic turned to devastation. My throat tightened, but I was determined not to cry, to stay optimistic for Lisa's sake, as well as my own. "It's OK," I said. "We'll just have to keep going. We'll make it."

I heard crying that night, and I, too, cried—as quietly as I could. I know that Lisa, exhausted beyond belief but unable to sleep because of the people squeezing on her from all sides, cried that night. We were so physically uncomfortable—there was no room to lie down, no room to sit, all of our hot and filthy bodies pressed tightly together for all those days. Added to that was this fresh disappointment, and we were beyond miserable. I drifted off to sleep, sporadically waking to hunger, thirst, and discomfort. I tried to muster some hope as the sun rose on the sixth day. There was no food, and our store of water was nearly depleted. I fantasized about digging into a big bowl of steaming rice, taking a bite of a sizzling pork chop. My mouth was too dry to salivate, but I imagined the sensation of a full stomach and tried to remember what it felt like to take a huge gulp of cold water and drink to my heart's content.

On the seventh day, we saw trash.

CHAPTER 6

Hope in the Philippines

I've never been so happy to see garbage in all my life. Garbage meant people, and people meant land.

Fighting for space at the side of the boat, we fixated on the trash as though the plastic bottles and empty soda cans were tea leaves at the bottom of a teacup that foretold our future. Some of the passengers cheered and hugged. I no longer had to muster hope—it was there, in this beautiful pile of floating trash. Maybe we'd make it after all.

A few hours later, a black dot of land came into view. We were almost there.

Just as the shape of land came into view, a small fishing boat approached, manned by five big Filipino guys in swimsuits. They offered us water, and at first, we were too hungry and thirsty to be suspicious. It was common knowledge that, at that time, more raiders roamed the South China Sea by Thailand, so we'd gone in the opposite direction, toward the Philippines, in hopes of avoiding them. You could never know who was a friend and who wasn't, so there was nothing to do but accept their help gratefully and hope for the best. They were very friendly, and after we'd each taken a drink, they asked for some money. No big deal—we all chipped in to come up with a few hundred bucks and a ring. "Let's get you tied up to our boat," one of the men said, "and then we can tow you in."

Our lives were saved! We'd survive!

Then, after the boats were tied together, one of the men took out a shotgun, and they started dragging us in the opposite direction, away from land. At first, what was happening didn't quite click for any of us.

"Hey there," the captain called to them. "Where are you going?"

They ignored him.

"Hey!" The rest of us joined in the yelling. "Hey, stop!" One of the guys turned around and yelled at us to shut up. He picked up the gun and held it where we could see it, and a quiet panic spread across the boat. What could we do? We had nothing, no weapons. What if they robbed us, then let us go? What if they took some of the women? What if they killed us?

"We have to cut the rope," someone whispered.

"But what if they shoot us?" came another whisper.

"They'll run out of bullets eventually."

"Are you volunteering to be the one to get shot?"

We were so weak by this point, nearly delirious with hunger and thirst, that we were unable to think clearly, let alone fight back if it came to that. Our fates were entirely out of our control, in the hands of these strange men with a gun.

By some miracle, another boat pulled up. It was a much fancier vessel than ours or the other one, and it was obvious from the way its owner wore his well-tailored suit that he was a big shot. Next to him stood two mean-looking bodyguards with two mean-looking machine guns. "Help!" we yelled, waving our arms. "Please, help us!"

"We're trying to get to the Philippines," a guy who spoke English shouted. "These guys are trying to kidnap us!"

The big shot quickly assessed the situation, then addressed the aspiring pirates in Tagalog. He ordered them to untie us, and what could they do but obey? The bodyguards' machine guns left no room for disagreement. Once they'd driven off, the big shot said in English, "Don't worry, we'll take you in." We waited while he radioed someone; we didn't know who. Then we followed behind his fancy boat toward the shore.

We made it to land just before dark. The sunset was casting an orange light across the shallows as our boat pulled in. I cannot begin to describe the relief, the joy, the immense gratitude that overtook me as we all spilled out into the water. Seven days and nights we'd been at sea, and our sea legs would need to adjust to walking on land. On the beach, I dropped to my knees like so many others alongside me, and kissed the ground, grains of sand sticking to my dry lips. I ran my hands over the beach's white warm surface, knelt down, and pressed my cheek into it, then simply lay down. I rolled over onto my back and looked up at the sky, tears streaming from my eyes and running down my temples and into the sand. Others were crying and jumping up and down. "Land!" we cried. "We made it!" We'd been so close to death so many times, and this was life. We'd escaped Vietnam; this was our dream come true. We'd arrived.

***

Talampulan Island is a tiny tropical island about 180 miles southwest of Manila, just off the coast of Busuanga Island. The people of Talampulan were warm and generous, very different from the pirates we'd just escaped. The local authorities met us at the beach and took us to a huge warehouse. Underneath the high metal ceiling, we lay down on the floor to sleep.

The next morning, I awoke and walked outside to a bright blue sky. The temperature was perfect, not too hot or humid. Volunteers brought us used clothes to replace our clothing, which had become salt-encrusted rags during the voyage. I pulled my "brand-new" T-shirt over my head. It was clean and soft and smelled like nothing, in that moment the most delicious scent in the world.

We milled about, hungry and unsure of what to do next. One of the locals stopped in to the warehouse to announce that a fishing boat had just arrived. We followed her down to the pier, too excited to worry about not having any baskets to carry the fish in. Without thinking, I stripped off my T-shirt and, holding it stretched between my hands like a net, reached out to the boat over the water—putting some meat back on my bones was more important than covering them. I didn't quite realize that this would be the only shirt I'd receive for a while, and I'd have to spend the next few days smelling like fish.

When we got back to the warehouse, there was fresh bread waiting, its aroma filling the warehouse. Lisa and Hang had gone to the bakery, which happened to be owned by a Chinese family, and they'd been kind enough to share, no charge. I'll never forget that meal—we hadn't eaten in a week, and nothing had ever tasted so good.

For a few days, we were free to do nothing but walk around, sit under palm trees, get a bite to eat, get our land legs back. I sent a telegram home to let my family know that we were alive. Lisa and Hang got a ride on a local's bike to the town center, where they were able to get some toothpaste and soap. I visited the trusty boat that had taken us such a long distance and found it dead in the water.

"The engine's dead," someone told me. "It did its job." *Rest in peace*, I thought. On the third day, I was walking around down by the pier when I saw a guy on a bike with a pot of stew. It smelled heavenly, and I bought a little bowlful of it. The next time I saw him, he was chasing a dog. Putting two and two together, I realized that the meat in the stew had been dog. And it was delicious.

Every now and then, I'll look back at the few photos we have from that time, taken by a fellow refugee whose family had managed to send him a camera. Hang, our friend Tran and his six-year-old son, Lisa, and I look so young, so thin in our donated Adidas, Esprit, and Puma T-shirts, and yet we look happy, standing under a palm tree and drinking Coke out of glass bottles. Those pictures bring to mind the relief we felt more than the pain and suffering that came before. They're a testament to our resilience—and youth—and we were able to look forward with hope, optimism, and openness.

A week into our stay on the island, we took a boat to Palawan Refugee Camp. Upon arrival, all 143 of us lined up to check in, just like you'd do at a fancy hotel. But, as you'd expect, the Palawan Refugee Camp was nothing fancy. It was huge, however, divided into districts and with enough room for eighteen thousand people, and it had the amenities of a small city—schools, hospitals, libraries, markets, even restaurants and sports facilities. I was surprised to learn that some of the refugees had been there for upward of ten years, just killing time waiting for sponsorship. Sometimes these refugees-in-limbo would get fed up and escape, trying to blend into the regular Filipino population, with varying degrees of success.

I was even more surprised to find out just how lucky we had been. While awaiting housing assignments, we stayed in a holding cell where we swapped stories with our fellow new arrivals. "Seven days?" someone said, scoffing. "We were out there ten days." "Yeah," said someone else, "we were out fourteen." The stories we heard were unbelievable, horrific, beyond anything I could've imagined. Pirates had boarded ships to rape and murder and kidnap. Many people had died of thirst or starvation or sunstroke. Some, in absolute desperation, had resorted to cannibalism. Some boats had created a lottery system to pick who would be eaten; others would simply prey on the weak. The worst story I heard happened over the course of a sixty-day voyage. A group of strong, young men had banded together, taking it upon themselves to pick off people one by one to kill with their bare hands and eat. Compared to that, our boat trip had been a pleasure cruise.

The holding cell was like a cage, with wooden bars and a mud floor. It was also sort of like a market: every day, the established refugees would walk by and peer in, examining us newly arrived refugees, the merchandise. They were looking for two kinds of people—strong men who could fight and pretty girls—to join their households. At all times, we were on our best behavior, trying to somehow convey our friendly dispositions and love of hard work. Pretty soon, a Chinese Vietnamese person came around, and, recognizing our common ethnic background, picked us out of the crowd. This included me and Lisa plus Uncle Tran and his son and Hang.

The open-air, bamboo two-story huts that we lived in had thatched roofs and ladders between floors. With very little room, we somehow managed to fit ten or twelve of us into a single structure. The ladder led to a flat bamboo landing, where everyone slept on mats on the floor. At night, we fell asleep to the sound of waves crashing on the shore. As nice as that sounds, with no walls, there was no privacy. This was true for the camp as a whole. The only spot in the house that had even the possibility of privacy was the one bedroom off the main room of the floor where we cooked and shared meals and hung out together. That one room was generally occupied by the resident with the most seniority. When we first moved in, one woman, her sister, and her sister's husband all shared it. A few months later, a baby joined them, the son of the unmarried sister. We threw them a little party to welcome the newest arrival, born in a refugee camp far from any kind of home. He was a happy addition, though I never did learn who the father was. We all chipped in to help the new mom out, because that's just what you did.

In a place where you could hear every sound, we kept our voices low out of consideration, but try asking that of a newborn! There was more than one night when his cries woke me, but he was pretty cute with his big dark eyes and tousled hair, and so easy to forgive. Along with not caring too much about privacy, adaptability was very important. Within our little household, we all got along for the most part.

People were always coming and going as some left and others arrived. Pretty soon, the two sisters, husband, and baby moved out, so I got to choose some new housemates. This happened many times over the course of the year, and every time we took stock of the qualities that an ideal housemate should have. He or she would be friendly yet not too friendly, hardworking yet relaxed, independent but not bossy. We wanted people who could pull their weight when it came to household chores, but who wouldn't be too uptight, since there was really no way to hold back the disarray caused by constant flux.

Along with the human tenants, we'd ended up taking in a stray cat—or, rather, a stray cat had decided to grace us with his presence. You know how cats are. He was a skinny little thing, his fur white with a few black spots along his back. We did not even give him a name, but he was a welcome addition to the household. During meals, each of us took turns giving him a morsel or two of our small rations. He would purr and rub his scruffy little body against our legs, a little dose of affection that we were all starved for. Having that responsibility to care for something small and vulnerable got us through many long, boring days. We were all in limbo, waiting to pass our tests for tuberculosis, learn English, and get our paperwork cleared so that we could go live with whichever relative had sponsored us. Most of us had sponsors in the United States or Canada, and we were hoping to start new lives very soon in that distant part of the world. Some people took drugs or drank, but I avoided falling back into old habits. We weren't allowed to work outside the camp, so the only money I had came from my uncles and aunties who had previously escaped Vietnam and relocated to different parts of the world, and I didn't want to waste their generosity on cigarettes or booze.

My one job was to get water, which took up a significant part of each day. On-site, there were only well water and a public fountain, which the more than one hundred households in District 1 used. It took two or three hours to get through the line for water, and I'd make the short walk every day, wait in line, fill some buckets, and carry them back, then repeat the process all over again. Not everyone had the capacity to do this, so most people used the public fountain to take showers and wash their clothes. But I wanted to make sure that our house—and Lisa, in particular—could bathe and do laundry in privacy.

On top of that, every day we'd spend an hour or two waiting in line to trade in our vouchers for food that would be our breakfast, lunch, and dinner. I also spent two hours a day learning English in the big cement building that we used as a schoolhouse. Now that I could imagine a real future ahead, I was very motivated. I knew that, in order to succeed in my new life, I'd need to master the language of my new country—which I hoped would be Canada.

The rest of my days were wide open, and I spent those empty hours swimming in the ocean, which was just on the other side of the camp's wall. I jumped it at least two or three times a day to get into those waves.

My life was eating, studying, fetching water, swimming, and sleeping. Sometimes a group of us would kick a soccer ball around, or go shrimping in the middle of the night. Looking back, in a way it seems like a vacation. I think that a lot of us very busy people might eye that situation with something like envy. But I can tell you for sure that at the time, it definitely didn't feel like a vacation—we were all in limbo, just waiting to leave and get on with our lives.

Of course, with so many people crammed into the camp, all nervously awaiting new lives, there was bound to be some friction. Plus, with so much free time, there were plenty of opportunities to get into a scuffle, whether it was because someone had cut in line for water or food, or someone thought someone else had taken more than their fair share, or someone gave someone else a funny look. The reason wasn't all that important—as they say, idle hands are the devil's playthings, and at least fighting was something to do. Fights broke out nearly every week, and if

I was good at one thing besides making friends, it was making enemies. I was never afraid to throw some punches, though my Kung Fu training made it so I'd always wait until someone threw one first. That way I could claim it was self-defense!

One day, I got up as usual to go for my early-morning swim. I went outside, expecting to see the usual panoramic view just above the camp wall, the beach and the ocean glowing golden in the sunrise, the sky a mix of pink and blue. Instead, I found myself looking straight into the eyes of the cat. He was on the wall, staring at me. I tilted my head, rubbed the sleep out of my eyes. He didn't move. I stepped forward, and my breath caught in my throat. It was the cat's head all right, but where his body was—that was a mystery.

I freaked out. *I'm going to kill the bastard who did that to my cat,* I thought. "I am going to kill you, you bastard!" I yelled at the top of my lungs. There were creaks and groans from the inside of the house, and then Lisa and the others were standing beside me. "The cat!" I pointed. "The freakin' cat!"

I had too many enemies to narrow down the suspects. And the cat had belonged to the whole house, so it could've been a message for someone else. Or it could've been a jerk who was bored and had nothing better to do than decapitate an innocent animal. I'll never know who hurt that poor kitty, and that is a mental image and a heartache that, even after so many years, I just can't seem to shake.

***

Fortunately, it wasn't all boredom-inspired fighting or troublemaking inside the camp. With so much free time, Lisa and I had a chance to get to know each other. She was busier than I was, however. Because of her language proficiency, the French and Filipino governments hired her to teach French and English classes, and the UN hired her to work as an interpreter. She translated between the refugees and the UN representatives who were interviewing them to determine their status. Quickly, she realized the ideal they were going for: a young, healthy person who was willing to work, knew English, and could prove that they had been persecuted by the Vietnamese government. They would ask, "Why have you left your country?" If the reply was, "We had nothing. We had no food, no way to make a living, and we were starving," they would be denied asylum because this was considered an economic reason, not a political one. If you were Chinese, considered an intellectual, or branded as an enemy of Vietnam, that would be enough. After Lisa told me this, I made sure to say that my dad had been a soldier who'd fought with the United States, and that the communists considered us the bad guys.

Still, it only took two months for me to fall head over heels for her. She was so smart, so far above me in so many ways. While I was just hanging around, she was doing something, helping people. I was willing to do anything for this tiny, intelligent woman, and I told her right away—I was never one to mince words or hold back my feelings.

"I like you," I said. We were in the open space of the second story of our house, and for the moment no one was around. I gave her a quick kiss on the cheek, to see what she'd do. She didn't respond in the affirmative, but she didn't say no, either. "I love you," I said the next day, and the one after that. She kept not responding but also not rejecting me, which was not the ideal response, but it was better than a flat-out no. I knew that I was probably not what she was looking for—she was more educated, more polite, nicer. She probably was thinking, *Oh, how sweet, but he'll get over it.* In fact, I'm pretty sure she didn't take me seriously one bit. That is, she didn't until she went out with a real jerk—a nicely dressed dork with lots of money sent by his relatives—and I couldn't contain myself. I'm telling you, I was *mad,* and I didn't try to hide it. When he brought her some fancy chocolate, I took it and threw it into the ocean. After that, she didn't go out with anyone else, and I think that's when she started to take the hint that my feelings were real.

I also began to go out of my way to impress her, take care of her, protect her. I wanted her to see that I could be responsible when I put my mind to it. Lisa was picky about food, and the food in the camp was not so good. We'd have four days straight of fish, with some pork or a can of sardines thrown into the mix every now and then. She couldn't bear to waste it. So, gentleman that I am, I ate every single bite of her leftovers. For whatever reason, she really appreciated that. With the little bit of money from my relatives plus what she earned through her job, we had some extra to spare. In the evenings, we'd go to the canteen that was expensive enough so that most refugees couldn't afford it; the Western volunteers were its primary customers. I wanted to save my money as best I could, so I'd buy some noodles or other camp delicacy for her, and nothing for myself. "I'm not hungry," I'd say. "You go ahead."

I'm pretty sure that over time she started to fall in love with me, too. But that didn't mean she accepted me—she was a much more traditional person, and back then, the age, education, and class differences between us mattered a lot. I'd just have to prove myself worthy of her, no matter what it took.

***

About six months after our arrival, Lisa left for the Philippine Refugee Processing Center (PRPC) with the other United States–bound refugees. There she would learn about American culture and get her physical exams. Meanwhile, I stayed behind while I waited for my sponsorship to Canada to come through. I knew that I loved her before she left, but I didn't realize just how much I loved her until she was gone. I missed her so much, that hungry, desperate, almost weepy feeling that happens when you're young and in love. I wrote her a love letter every day, then saved them up to be delivered in a batch by someone who was going to Bataan. *I really miss you,* I'd write. *I've never felt this way before.* She didn't write back as often as I wrote to her, but later she admitted that she had looked forward to receiving my letters. At the same time, she took my declarations of love with a grain of salt—later, in one of her more candid moments, she confessed that she thought we were never going to see each other again. *We're opposites,* she'd thought. *I'm a pessimist and he's an optimist. He doesn't know anything about responsibility and takes nothing seriously, and I'm serious about life.* Though she had feelings for me, she assumed that, after some time and distance, we'd eventually forget about each other.

I was determined not to let that happen. Four months after Lisa left, I escaped. Well, "escaped" isn't really the right word, since we were allowed to leave during the day, as long as we returned before curfew. I didn't "escape" so much as I left and didn't come back. Given that the refugee camp was full to capacity, what were the odds that anyone would even notice that I was gone?

It was a two-day, two-night ferry trip through Manila and on to Bataan. I arrived in Manila late, and there was no bus to Bataan. I had no money for a hotel, so I crawled through the fence of the Manila Transition Center when I got there and slept on the ground for the night. We'd stayed there for a few days before being transferred to Palawan, so I already knew my way around.

I stayed at the Bataan refugee camp with Lisa for one week. What was one more refugee among a thousand others? I had no problem blending in and no worries about anyone noticing my absence back in Palawan. Had I been caught, I could've been sent back to Vietnam, and everything I'd been through—the thirst, the hunger, the fear, the sickness—would have been in vain. I could have been executed as soon as I stepped foot on Vietnamese soil. But I think we can all agree that love makes us do crazy things, and I was willing to risk everything for this woman.

It was worth it. I think the fact that I had gone to such lengths softened Lisa. We had a wonderful week together, eating and catching up. Then she received a telegram from a friend at the camp in Palawan. Apparently, while I was gone, the doctor had come to give physical exams. Every day over the loudspeaker, they'd called my name. Talk about bad timing! I was, the friend informed us, in big, big trouble. The camp officials had even called my family in Canada! Of course, they did not know why I was missing.

Oh shit, I thought.

Lisa arranged for me to call my family to let them know where I was. During this time, my grandparents had miraculously been granted sponsorship and gone directly from Vietnam to their son's home in Canada. That was where I reached my grandmother. She was pissed.

"Do you want to get sent back to Vietnam?" my grandmother yelled.

After reassuring them that I was heading back to Palawan, I hung up, my ears still ringing. Lisa immediately picked up the phone and called a friend at the Manila camp to ask if they would give me my physical exam there. She was able to pull some strings because, as a highly sought-after translator, she'd earned some favors.

Back in Palawan, an official, wagging his finger in my face, threatened to put me in jail. Again, Lisa pulled some strings so that I could avoid this fate. Now, she truly owned my heart.

Around the same time, one year after our arrival in the Philippines, her sponsorship to the United States and my sponsorship to Canada came through. Not only would we be in different countries, but we'd also be on opposite coasts, me on the West Coast and she on the East Coast. I had my aunt, uncle, and cousin waiting for me, while she had a younger brother whom she hadn't seen in almost ten years. There were just too many unknowns ahead of us, and so even though we planned to stay in touch, Lisa wanted to put off figuring out the details.

"Let's just get to the other side first," she said.

CHAPTER 7

Prince Rupert

In March of 1989, I returned to Manila, then flew to Prince Rupert, British Columbia. Going from Manila to Vancouver was a big deal—finally my dream was coming true. It was my first time on an airplane, and even though I knew I was safe, a part of me was scared, plus nervous, excited, confused, anxious, and happy—all these feelings mixed together. I looked out the window, watching the ocean and the clouds sweep by, with no idea what lay ahead and thinking, just, *Wow.*

Back in Vietnam, I'd watched movies set in New York, Las Vegas, and Los Angeles. I'd seen the vibrant colors of Disneyland and Times Square, the bright blue of the sky and the deep yellow of the desert brush growing around the base of the Hollywood sign. *That is the American dream. Or heaven,* I thought. *Bright lights, big cities.*

I didn't know the distinction between the United States and Canada—to me, it was all "America." I landed in Vancouver and then, after completing the paperwork, immediately boarded another plane to Digby Island. After arriving, I walked to the bus parked near the terminal. The day was gray and, to me, very cold, Canada's version of early spring. To eyes used to bright tropical greens and purples and blues, the dark greens and browns and yellows looked muted. The airport was a ghost town—not a soul in sight except my fellow passengers, the two flight attendants, and the bus drivers waiting by their buses. The plane I'd just left was the only plane in the airport. *OK*, I thought as I boarded the bus. *This is a small town, but who knows what Prince Rupert is like? Maybe that's where the action is.*

After a short ride, the bus drove onto a ferry. Fifteen minutes later, we pulled up to the small commercial area of downtown Prince Rupert. It was not what I was expecting. There was not a giant neon-lit billboard in sight, no skyscrapers, no loud music or honking cars. It was quiet, really quiet, and the buildings were short and plain. Without a word, the other passengers took their luggage and disappeared. I got off the bus and scanned the area, feeling disappointed and totally lost. Luckily, there was a counter with an official-looking woman sitting behind it. I approached her, and, in my broken English, said something along the lines of, "I am a refugee. I have just arrived." I handed her the piece of paper with my uncle's home phone number. She took it and dialed, talked for a minute, then hung up. "He said, 'See you in a couple minutes,'" she reported.

Two minutes later, a little boy—my cousin, Shimmer, whom I'd never met—rode up on his bike and screeched to a halt in front of me. Uncle Nam, my mother's younger brother, arrived less than a minute later in a station wagon. I was confused and a little bit sad; I'd expected to be overjoyed but didn't feel happy one bit. I'd risked my life to get to Canada only to find that my uncle lived a couple minutes away from the bus terminal? This Canada was not at all the big city I'd envisioned. *Why am I here?* I asked myself. *I could've had a better life if I'd stayed in Vietnam.*

Still, a part of me knew that I had every reason to be grateful. I just needed some time to rest, to adapt and get settled, then I'd feel better. Still, I couldn't shake the thought that my dream of America was nothing like what I saw before me.

The car ride was too short to do much catching up. I knew some of what my uncle Vinh, uncle Nam and aunt Binh, and their son, Thuan, had been through since they left Vietnam in 1979, which was the last time I'd seen them. They, like so many boat people, had had an incredibly tough journey. Instead of heading east toward the Philippines, their boat, loaded with almost two hundred people, had gone south and managed to land in Malaysia, where the passengers disembarked and established a camp on an unused piece of land roughly the size of a football field. They were soon joined by other groups of refugees, and their numbers swelled. For one month they lived there, hundreds of people crammed into this tiny rectangle of space, hungry and dirty and helpless, until the Malaysian government forced them out.

Once back on the boat, they headed south, trying again and again to reach shore, only to have a Royal Malaysian Navy boat follow them along the coast to block their way at every turn. Three times they attempted to land; three times the navy boat tied them up and hauled them back out to sea.

Finally, the boat made it to Singapore, where they met a fisherman out fishing. He gave them water but told them, "The Singaporean government doesn't want you. Keep moving." So, they continued south, with very little water and no food. The Indonesian Navy did not give them a warm welcome, either—just off the coast, an enormous warship was waiting, prepared to turn away any attempts to land.

Finally, the old fishing boat was allowed through, to land on an uninhabited island to the east of the mainland. For two months, the refugees lived on that little island, surviving on canned pumpkin, rice, and fish sauce dropped by relief helicopters. They learned to catch fish using mosquito nets and how to find drinking water that washed into the creek when the tide went out. These were city dwellers, people who'd had no experience hunting, fishing, or surviving off the land. Eventually, they were moved to another island, where they lived in tents and ate the coconuts that fell from the trees, followed by a few months more in a sanctioned refugee camp.

St. Andrew's Cathedral in Prince Rupert had sponsored them, along with many other refugees. Nam, Binh, and their three-year-old son, Thuan, arrived in January. None of them had seen snow before, or experienced cold. The white powder along the rooftops seemed magical. They were immediately shown their new home, a furnished three-bedroom apartment. Aunt Binh had described their arrival by saying, "It was like going from hell to heaven." To this day, when she speaks of it, tears well up in her eyes. "We were welcomed by the church members. They were so warm, so kind. They asked, 'What do you need?' We answered, 'We need a job as soon as possible. We want to support ourselves.' They said, 'There's no hurry. Learn English first!' They kept asking the same question; we kept giving the same answer."

Uncle Nam got a job at a restaurant and Aunt Binh got a job as a babysitter within two weeks of landing. Little Thuan, weakened by months of hunger and thirst, was unable to recover from the journey and died soon after they arrived. To this day, we rarely talk about his death—this loss is a source of great sadness for all of us.

Uncle Nam and Aunt Binh worked and worked and worked, spending nothing, saving everything until, a couple years into their time in Prince Rupert, they were able to buy a house of their own. From their front porch, they watched the seasons change, saw the grass turn green and the flowers bloom as winter became spring. They had a son, Shimmer, that same year.

***

At the house, Aunt Binh was waiting for us on the front porch. She looked the same as I remembered her—small boned, wearing simple clothing, black hair neatly cut to frame her face. "Hao," she said, pulling me into a hug. "Welcome." Uncle Nam shot me the big grin I remembered, then gave me the grand tour. We walked through the living room to the kitchen, where I drank down a glass of water straight from the tap. He showed me the room in the basement where he and Aunt Binh slept, and Shimmer's and my grandparents' bedrooms on the main floor. The house was small but clean and tidy, with everything in its place. *Where am I going to sleep?* I wondered.

"Come on," my uncle said, "I'll show you your room." I followed behind him down the hallway, nearly bumping into him when he stopped abruptly. He reached up and popped a hatch in the ceiling above us. Then, using the walls for leverage, he shimmied up and into the hole. From where I stood, I couldn't see anything but a dark space.

His face suddenly popped out of the hole. "Come on," he said, "I converted the attic into a bedroom." I climbed up just as he had, though not quite as gracefully, then stood up and let my eyes adjust to the darkness. The space was tiny but cozy, with a bed, a bookshelf, a desk, and a heater. My uncle smiled. "This is your room." I felt a pressure behind my eyes. All that effort he'd gone to. I felt how much he cared, and for a moment, I felt guilty for the disappointment I'd felt at the bus station.

"Thank you, Uncle," I said.

The next day, Aunt Binh laid down the law, in her own soft-hearted way. It had been almost ten years since she'd seen me, and my guess is that my mom had told her and my uncle about my teenage troublemaking. "Hao," Aunt Binh said, "you are twenty-one years old now, an adult. I'm sorry to be so straightforward, but you are going to have to contribute to this household."

"Auntie," I said without hesitation, "I understand what I have to do."

For a few days I rested, and then my family showed me around. There wasn't much to see—the small "downtown" where the bus had dropped me off included a row of shops and restaurants. Prince Rupert Secondary School was southeast of the downtown and about a mile from the ocean, a frigid and dark place so different from the warm seas I was used to. There were towering evergreens everywhere, and without a doubt, there were more trees than people in the town.

Nam and Binh gave me some money and helped me to open a bank account. Uncle Vinh added a few hundred dollars to put into my account. They took me shopping for boots and a winter coat. No matter what, I was determined not to be a burden on my aunt and uncle. They were doing so much for me, and although it was not exactly what I'd envisioned, I was grateful for my new home.

That very first week, I tried to get a job as a jeweler, hoping to put the skills I'd learned from the master in Vietnam to good use. I impressed the jewelry-store owner in town with my ability to set a diamond, but I learned that I'd need a gemology certification—things were much more tightly regulated in Canada. The trip to Vancouver, the cost of the program, and the six months required to get the certification were three key things that I could not afford. Disappointed, I set aside my ego to ask my family for help finding a job.

***

Uncle Nam took me to meet Paul and Pam, the owners of Baker Boy Bakery, the town's only provider of freshly baked goods. That initial meeting went well, and the next day, I returned at noon as directed. I was so happy to get a job that I didn't ask about pay, or what exactly I'd be doing. I figured I'd be learning to bake. Paul, a first-generation Chinese Canadian who didn't know how to smile, handed me an industrial-size broom. "Welcome to your first day on the job," he said. "Now, sweep the floor."

The broom felt unreasonably heavy in my hands. I didn't cry—I wouldn't cry!—but I was crying on the inside. *Why am I here?* I asked myself again as I pushed the broom across the linoleum. *I used to be the boss—I gave that up for this?* Everyone has a job to do, we all have bills to pay, we all need to put food on the table. I respected people who did this kind of work. But I had been the big boss! I'd had my own business! I'd had a motorcycle! If I went back to Vietnam, I wouldn't have to sweep. I could've gone into the military, had everything paid for. OK, so I might be forced to fight my own people. And I wouldn't be free. But still! I'd risked my life to be a janitor? For me, a very proud young man, this was hard to take. What I mean to say is that it was a huge change, and along with day-old bread, I'd have to learn to eat some humble pie.

But that wouldn't happen for a while. That first night, I came home, climbed up to my attic room, and cried. I'd thought that going to North America meant going to heaven. The same thoughts kept running round and round in my head: *Why am I here? Why did I risk my life? This isn't the American dream. Where can I go from here as a janitor?*

I went back to work the next day. Every day from then on, I came in at noon, after the bakers had left, and cleaned up. Paul paid me a few hundred dollars a month—we'd never formalized this arrangement, and I didn't know anything about minimum wage or clocking hours. That just wasn't how it was done in Vietnam. I'd always paid my employees per shift, a shift lasting as long as the electricity was running. He probably took advantage of me, but what were my other options?

Sweeping floors every day gave me a lot of time to think about my plans. I decided that I needed—and wanted—an education. In September of 1989, six months after I'd arrived in Prince Rupert, I told my uncle that it was my dream to finish high school. I was twenty-one years old. Since he'd only known me as the uneducated and uninterested boy I'd been in Vietnam, this surprised him. But he took me to Prince Rupert Secondary School to meet with a guidance counselor, Mrs. Steward.

Her office was small and full of shelves holding books and binders. "Please, take a seat," she said, gesturing to the chairs in front of her desk. She sat down behind it. "Welcome to Canada. First things first. You'll have to take a test to prove your proficiency in English. Since you're over eighteen, the government will only provide funding for one year of schooling. That means you'll need to optimize your time here; you'll start in the twelfth grade, and for that you'll need sixty-five percent to pass."

I took the test. Of course, I did not pass.

"Your language is not good enough yet," she informed me. "I recommend that you go to Northwest Community College to get caught up." I was disappointed, but I promised her that I'd be back. "I look forward to seeing you again," she said.

And so, I enrolled in English and math at NWCC. I carried a Chinese-English dictionary with me everywhere. At first, I tried to use just the English side but found that that was way above my level, so instead I flipped back and forth between the Chinese and the English. I studied super hard, with the incredible support of my math teacher, John, and English teacher, Marie. At night, after a long day of floor scrubbing at the bakery, I went to see a volunteer mentor, an optometrist named Myrna, who had three sons around my age. I'd go to her store after they closed, and we'd have conversations in English.

Along with wanting to pass the proficiency test, I also wanted to make more money. I got a second job washing dishes at Imperial Palace, the Chinese restaurant next door to the bakery. There I found out about the concept of an hourly wage. Like the schedule of most immigrants trying to build a life in a new country, my days were very full—I went to school in the morning, cleaned the bakery from noon until three o'clock, washed dishes until past midnight, and somehow squeezed in time to meet with Myrna and study.

Though I mostly did menial tasks at the bakery, I sometimes came in early to help the bakers, pulling sandwiches out of the oven while suffering the industry-standard burns up and down my arms and inhaling flour until I coughed up white clouds. This being a small town, the baker guarded the secrets of his recipes, so I never did learn much about baking. Instead, I set piping-hot dinner rolls, apple turnovers, donuts, and donut cakes on metal racks to cool. I salivated over the apple and blueberry strudels, bagged bread and pastry, and drove around town to make deliveries to the corner store, the gas station, the local restaurants, and the supermarket. If a sandwich or pastry wasn't perfect, I'd get to eat it, and, every now and then, Pam's mom would bring in a home-cooked meal. At the restaurant, I filled my belly with leftover Chinese food late at night after I'd finished washing dishes. My bones started to get a healthy little layer of fat on them. Though I was interested in learning to cook, I wasn't given the opportunity. Again, the small-town chefs didn't want to train what could be the competition, so they kept their skills to themselves. I did learn to cut vegetables and mushrooms and clean meat, which came in handy at home. Sometimes Imperial Palace catered wedding banquets, and I'd stay out until one or two o'clock in the morning, washing a mountain of wedding cake- and spicy beef–encrusted dishes, spraying the plates and glasses and loading and unloading the tiny dishwasher over and over again until my hands chapped and bled and my back ached.

Sometimes I slept. I thought I could handle going to school and working two jobs, but eventually work took its toll. One night, at a wedding banquet, the dishes kept coming in nonstop, and I washed and washed and washed until dawn. That was the final straw—I could barely get my tired body home before passing out into a dreamless sleep. I basically slept for two days straight. Still, I didn't have the option of feeling sorry for myself. Most immigrants don't get spa days or "me time."

Whenever I was feeling down or disappointed, I'd think of Lisa. She was the main reason I was working so hard, to show that I was worthy of her and to prepare for the life I hoped we would share. I also thought of her because, as I learned from our phone calls, compared to her life, mine was a cakewalk.

***

Lisa had arrived in New York City in May of 1989, about two months after I landed in Prince Rupert. Unlike me, she hadn't had a warm reception and a support system in place. Her younger brother picked her up at the airport, and that same evening— even though Lisa had spent more than fifteen hours travelling from the Philippines to New York—he wanted her to stay up listening to his story. To Lisa's surprise, he was miserable, furious, and resentful. For the previous ten years, he had written letters home once in a while, though not often; he did send gifts home like other Vietnamese sons and daughters who had left home. But he never mentioned how bad the situation was, maybe because there was nothing they could've done had they known, except worry.

"Do you know how miserable the last ten years have been for me?" he said. "Why did Mom send me? Why did you all abandon me?"

Lisa tried to explain their intentions—that their mother and sisters all thought they were doing the best for him. He was the only son in the family, and they were willing to sacrifice all their money to send him out to find a good future.

"All I know is I was alone," he replied. "I saw homeless people living in subway stations, but they had their kids with them, and I wondered, how come I am alone? Do you know that I had to sleep at the subway station by myself? I want you to walk the same path I did. I want you to go through the same hardships so that you will understand what I have been through."

Lisa did not blame him, even when he told her to move out a couple of months later when she got a full-time job at Lutheran Immigration and Refugees Service (LIRS) as a social worker. But she felt helpless to mend the relationship between them. He was hurt so much that he did not believe the love, compassion, and kindness shown to him by others—even his own sister.

It was an incredible struggle for Lisa. She worked full-time at LIRS and went to college in the evening, not to mention learning to navigate a new system in a new country, especially hard in a big city like New York. But the most difficult challenge she faced was to figure out how to help her brother, who seemed to have psychological problems. She believed it was her duty to take care of her brother and her family back in Vietnam. She had to stay strong physically and financially to have the ability to support her brother and sponsor her family to come over from Vietnam.

We kept in touch over the phone, and sometimes all I could do was listen to her cry. I felt so bad for her—I wished that I could be by her side, but all I could do was listen.

CHAPTER 8

Born-Again Student

That first year flew by. My uncle Nam had been trying to sponsor my parents for years, but siblings (and siblings-in-law) aren't considered immediate family and so are lower down on the immigration priority list. My grandparents had sponsored me, and now that I'd made it, I was, as immediate family, able to update the paperwork and speed up the process. Uncle Nam was still their financial sponsor, and he arranged a house for us for when they arrived.

Almost two years after I had landed, I returned to the bus station to welcome my parents and my sister, Kitty. I tried not to pace as my aunt, uncles, cousin, grandparents, and I waited for them in the quiet, gray terminal. Finally, the sound of the engine announced the bus, which pulled up and stopped, then opened its doors with a whoosh. A couple of unfamiliar people disembarked, and then, after a moment, my dad, followed by my sister and mom. They looked tired and rumpled from the journey, but as soon as they saw us, they waved, smiling broadly. I ran over to them and clasped their hands, each in turn.

"Welcome," I said. "I am so overjoyed that you are here."

The four of us moved into our new place, and I, with my own year of experience in Canada, helped them get settled. I showed them around town, giving them a tour of the grocery store and the drugstore, taking them to the Chinese restaurants. For the first time in many years, we had dinners together, sitting around the kitchen table over bowls of rice and vegetables, the sauce thicker than what we'd had in Vietnam. At first, I asked them all kinds of questions about what they'd been doing while I was gone, how our friends were, how the neighborhood had changed in my absence. Both my sister and I had grown up in the time we'd been apart, and suddenly we had lots to talk about. We became much closer than we had been before.

Then, it was time for me to retake the English test. This time, I passed.

I was beyond thrilled. Finally, I'd get to make up for my reckless waste of schooling in Vietnam. I'd get to be a kid again, but this time I'd get to find out what the learning environment was all about. I would be older than everyone else, but I still looked young, and I hoped that I would be able to fit in.

I returned to Northwest Community College to tell my teachers the good news and to say, "Sayonara!" I was fully expecting them to be as happy for me as I was for myself, but instead, each in turn said, "You should stay here at the college and get your GED."

"No," I replied, "it's my dream to go to high school. I want to be a student." And with that, I left NWCC. Back at Prince Rupert Secondary School, the counselor, Mrs. Koziski, who was also an English teacher, detailed the courses I'd need to graduate. It was going to be a push, since I was so far behind, and though my language skills had improved, I was nowhere near fluent. Still, I was confident that I could do it.

Most of the kids had gone to school together since kindergarten, and very few of them were immigrants or refugees like me. Fortunately, I had a second cousin named Quan Quan who attended the school. He showed me around and introduced me to his good friends, Diane and Janet. The three of them became my high school circle.

I took both English 11 and 12 at the same time, plus math and biology. If I had to guess, I'd say that I probably studied five times harder than the other students. I needed that Chinese-English dictionary in my hands every second of every day just to make it through my classes. On top of that, I was still determined to continue making money, so I switched to working evenings at a fast food restaurant at the Rupert Square Mall. The owner of No. 1 Fast Foods Center (which is still around today) was a wonderful guy by the name of Alan Chan. He and his wife, Margaret, who worked at the register at the restaurant, were both very nice. They treated all their employees well and kept the working atmosphere light and casual, a contrast to the environment at Baker Boy Bakery. Alan wasn't possessive of his cooking secrets, and from him I learned the Canadian classics—fish-and-chips, hamburgers, that sort of thing. Chow mein, too. I also learned from Alan's brother, Alec, who owned a fancier restaurant called the Anchorage. He taught me to cook some incredible meals, more upscale Canadian classics like seafood, lasagna, and steak. But I saw how his business struggled; there were some nights he didn't have a single customer. In Alan and Margaret, though, I had a model of what a boss should be—kind and organized, able to maintain a balance between running a business and caring for employees. Alan also owned a second business—the biggest catering company in town. I'd help out with that, too, donning a chef's hat at wedding receptions and standing at the banquet to cut prime rib or honey ham, which were kept warm under the pink glow of the heat lamp. Sometimes a teacher or classmate, dressed to the nines, would approach and ask, "Can I get medium rare?" before looking up and recognizing me. It was a little awkward in the beginning, at least for me—I felt strange being the server rather than a guest. But I still had a good time, and sometimes I'd go home with extra cash in my pocket.

After the party, we'd clean the venue, pack up everything, and haul it back to the restaurant. Then Alan would take us out for a meal at one of the few local restaurants that stayed open late. I couldn't afford to eat out, so this was a huge treat. Between those meals and the leftovers I got to take home from weddings, working for Alan kept me well fed. There were even enough leftovers to feed my family. My aunt Binh refused to take any money from me, always telling me to save it for school when I offered it. But at least I could share the leftovers—in this small way, I was able to contribute.

***

Math was something of a life raft in that ocean of English. I loved math, and I was good at it. So good that neighborhood parents hired me—sometimes with pay, sometimes not—to tutor their kids. After school, I rode my bike to their houses, receiving a dollar or two every now and then. Like at my bakery job, I didn't make a formal arrangement. I didn't attempt to negotiate. After all, I didn't have any money to spare, so even seven dollars was a lot. Plus, I was discovering that I had not only a knack for teaching but a passion for it, and spending time with the kids was its own reward.

Quickly word spread in our small town, and I developed a good reputation as a math tutor. At my high school, Mrs. Koziski introduced me to the head of tutoring, who offered me class credit in exchange for helping the other students. In her office at lunch, I set up shop as a tutor, which allowed me to practice English and make some friends at the same time. I may not have been the best at math in my class, but I was, it turns out, the best at *teaching* math.

Pretty soon my reputation grew, and the guidance counselor asked me if I would be willing to tutor the students for the provincial math exam. I agreed and received two keys to the high school—one to the outside door of the school building and one to a classroom. Sure, I no longer had a motorcycle and the status that went along with it, but for me, as a born-again student, this was just as good, if not better.

The first evening session, I expected just a few people to show up. There were only two grade twelve math classes at PRSS. To my surprise, fifteen minutes before class, the room was already packed. All the seats were taken, and at least half a dozen students were standing by the windows or leaning up against the wall at the back. I was very surprised and very nervous. Me, an old man (relatively) with limited English and no public speaking skills to, well, speak of—it was very intimidating!

Up there, in front of a bunch of students experiencing their own anxieties, I took a deep breath. I had a full belly, the beginnings of a life plan, and my freedom. I could do this.

For a couple of weeks, in my imperfect English, I taught test-taking strategies. "All you have to do is pass the test," I reminded them. "That's it. You don't have to be perfect—you don't even have to finish. Skip the problems you don't understand and come back to them later if you have time. Do what you know first. Use the process of elimination and other tricks and tips."

The students seemed to get a lot out of our strategy sessions, and, over time, I became more and more comfortable. I realized that teaching was in my blood. My mom was a teacher, after all. I must have learned to teach—patience, taking the time to explain, to listen—without being aware of it during those afternoons she tutored students at home. I enjoyed helping people, watching them go from being afraid of math and worried about the test to being relieved and calm by the end of our lesson.

At my graduation ceremony, I wore a stylish white tuxedo with a black cummerbund. I was so nervous and excited, thrilled to have finished what I'd worked so hard to do. After we'd all walked across the stage, the English teacher and counselor, Mrs. Koziski, Mrs. Stewart, and the math teacher, Ms. Stuart, called me back up on stage. The sound of my name being called a second time gave me a jolt, and with some effort I walked up the aisle and then up the stairs without tripping. In front of a hundred and twenty classmates and their families, the three teachers thanked me for my contribution and presented me with a graphing calculator. Back then, in 1991, those were super-duper cool—like a little computer! And they were expensive, costing around $200. The teachers had chipped in to buy the calculator for me out of pocket. I'd never received a gift this valuable and significant. I accepted it with tears in my eyes. I'd make good use of it, I promised myself.

***

As a twenty-three-year-old high school graduate, I was ready to start work and get married. To Lisa, of course. She was still in New York, still walking from neighborhood to neighborhood to visit the refugees assigned to her caseload. This was way before GPS, and so she carried a large paper map wherever she went. Despite her stressful life, somehow she found the energy to encourage me from a distance. She was the one who motivated me to go to school. She supported me on phone calls, and I was also determined to do anything to be at her level, to become worthy of her.

After graduating high school, I decided that college would be my next step, which was not necessarily expected of a refugee like me. People would ask me why I wanted to go to university, since I could easily get a job at the salmon cannery or the paper mill. There I could make good money, something like $20 an hour, which was very good pay in the 1990s. Plenty of my classmates had decided not to go to school, because there were so many good local union jobs. The average home in Prince Rupert cost around $45,000 (the equivalent of less than $100,000 today), a price they'd be able to afford after a few years earning that kind of salary.

What did I know about university? Nothing. So why would I bother getting a degree, when a decent job was available? Because I was determined to be worthy of Lisa. And, I reasoned, if the college thing didn't work out, the jobs would still be there.

The school counselor, however, told me that before I applied to the University of British Columbia, there were some things I'd need to take care of first. UBC required a transcript from grades nine through twelve, which obviously I didn't have. She recommended that, instead, I should go back to Northwest Community College and get a year's worth of transfer credits, Canada's version of an associate's degree. My friend Diane and I both signed up, and that fall, I was back at school. That year of classes was not super difficult. I took English, physics, and math. I had a really good college-level calculus teacher, who made the more abstract math relatively easy to comprehend. I continued flipping burgers part-time at No. 1 Fast Foods Center, serving classmates and teachers milk shakes, chow mein, and fish-and-chips whenever they came by. I also decided to take the skills I'd learned at my previous jobs and apply them in the kitchen at Irene Ma's Neptune Hotel. The hotel had around a hundred rooms, and Irene Ma hired me to be the only chef per shift, working alongside one or two waitresses. Sometimes we'd have fifty breakfast orders hit all at once, and we'd just have to make it happen as quickly as we could. I had lots of experience working in fast food, so the pace was no problem, but I'd never cooked so many different kinds of meals. I cooked the $1.99 breakfast special of two eggs over easy with bacon and toast, lovingly threw together a clubhouse, a BLT, a cheeseburger and fries, or my now-familiar fish-and-chips for lunch, and then prepared halibut cheek, steak sandwiches, and salmon entrées for dinner. I designed the lunch special every day after looking through the kitchen's stores and the big industrial refrigerator, while the more senior chef designed the dinner menu. I did the dishes, too, and sometimes I answered the phone and took reservations. Irene and I got along very well, and from her I learned a lot about the hospitality and food-service industry.

Sometimes my second cousin Quan Quan would recruit me to help him wash the Greyhound buses that ran between Vancouver and Prince Rupert. He had a contract that paid $9 or $10 per bus, and we'd split that for a whopping $4.50 apiece. Unsurprisingly, summer was not when he wanted my help—on a nice sunny day, he could handle the job just fine on his own. Who needs help when the sun is shining? Only on the coldest days would he ask me to come along. The most bitter days were actually easier—the water would freeze in the hose, and we wouldn't have to spray the bus because we couldn't. But we still got paid. The worst days were those that were cold enough to freeze our hands but not cold enough to freeze the hose, so we'd have to spray and soap up the sides and the roof, washing the bus inside and out as our fingers turned pink, then red, then blue. Cleaning up backseat vomit, scrubbing the bathrooms that people used on bumpy roads, scraping filth from the floors—that was hard work. But since my arrival, I'd grown less picky. I no longer had an ego about sweeping floors or rinsing off ice-cold bird poop while risking frostbite—I'd take any opportunity to make a few bucks.

***

School, work, more school, more work.

Sometimes I slept.

As the dark and icy winter transformed into a wet and chilly spring, I sent out applications to the University of British Columbia, the University of Victoria, and Simon Fraser University. I flipped burgers in my paper hat. I plated salmon and steak in my chef's apron. I still loved school and helping other students, but the thought of being a teacher had never even crossed my mind—I was a little guy in a little town, and even though I'd passed all my tests, I still considered my English to be subpar. So, my dreams stayed small, and I wasn't totally certain about how I'd do at university. Then, one morning toward the end of that year at community college, I was reading the newspaper and spotted a job opening for a position at the Prince Rupert branch of the sheriff's office. I instantly recalled my fantasies from childhood:

I still wanted to be that martial arts hero—strong, tough, protecting citizens. I applied and took the physical. I practiced for the special Class 4 driver's license, which I'd need because I'd be transporting people in one of those cool cop cars.

A couple of weeks later, I got a job offer to start part-time as a sheriff, and if everything worked out, it would eventually lead to a full-time position. I could be a hero! My multilingualism was actually considered an advantage, because they wouldn't need to hire a translator. The sheriff's office would send me to the Vancouver Police Academy right away to begin my training.

I called Lisa. "I got the job!" I said. "It pays eighteen dollars an hour, can you believe it? That's a lot of money! We can get married and start a family!"

"Huh," she said. "What about school?"

Coincidentally, at the same time, I got an acceptance letter from UBC.

I had a big decision to make. I placed the two acceptance letters on the kitchen table. A clock ticked somewhere in the house. Before me, on the wooden surface recently cleared of breakfast dishes and wiped clean, was my future, all the possibilities and the unknowns. I weighed the pros and cons:

1. Become a sheriff, sponsor Lisa so that she can come to Canada, get married, start a family, live happily ever after.
2. Go to university—and then?

Here's a quick summary of how my conversations about the decision went:

Friends and family: Take the job, it's a good job!

Lisa: Definitely go to school.

Me: No, I have to make money. I want to get married and start a family and support our relatives.

Friends and family: Take the job, it's a good job!

Lisa: If you go to school and finish and still can't get a job, you can be a sheriff. If you get a job now, you'll never go back to school.

I went to the sheriff's office to turn down the job offer.
"Go ahead," said the secretary. "He's in his office."
I knocked lightly on the door.
"Come in," the sheriff said. I opened the door and walked in, then shut it carefully before turning to face him. He sat behind his big desk, looking official and important in his starched uniform.
"I'm sorry, sir," I said. "I cannot accept the job offer. I am very grateful for the opportunity. But I have decided to go to university instead."
The boss was disappointed, but, more than that, he was irritated. I believe his exact words were "Are you out of your mind?"

CHAPTER 9

Fighting for Lisa

And so, I began to prepare myself for UBC. Now that I'd made one decision, a succession of new decisions stood before me. The biggest one was what my major was going to be. I wanted to avoid English because it was hard, but at the same time, I wanted to learn it and knew that in the long term, it would be in my best interest. After weighing the pros and cons, I decided to go for a BA in math, rather than a BS, because this would force me to take more English.

I wish that, at this juncture, someone had swooped in to give me some advice. But none of my family members had any idea what I should do, since I'd be the first of the family to go to college. I didn't know that there were professionals at the university whose job was to advise on this sort of thing—"academic advisor" was not yet part of my vocabulary.

If only someone had informed me that the engineering program would've allowed me to use my math skills in a more practical way. The same for business or computer science. I could've worked for Boeing or Microsoft straight out of college! I had no clue, and I would soon find out how little I could do with a bachelor's degree in math. I worked hard and believed in myself. I was uninformed but optimistic.

That first year I moved to campus, into the high-rise Walter Gage dorm. I shared a floor with twenty-four people, with six students per room. A lot of people from Hong Kong had recently flooded into Canada, and so many of my fellow students at UBC were ethnically Chinese. Quickly I made friends and formed a study group so I could maintain my tutoring skills. And yes, I'll admit, I wanted to show off a bit. I thought I was one of the best students, and everyone back in Prince Rupert had loved my teaching. Not just any student had been given a fancy calculator at graduation.

My ego was coming back—that is, until some of the people in my study group started getting better grades than I got. I was pissed! My grades were a big point of pride, and I was embarrassed about being so sure of myself in the teaching role but not having the grades to back it up. I was even getting a $500 scholarship because I'd declared my plan to study education so that I could eventually teach math. I think that, because of that confidence, I got careless and went too fast during the tests. Throughout my schooling, I got one C. In Chinese. My own language. That's so embarrassing to admit! To this day, I tell my students, "I don't care how well you think you know the material; you have to slow down, calm down, take your time." I learned that lesson the hard way.

***

That first year, I studied like a demon.

During the four-month summer break, I returned to Prince Rupert to work two full-time jobs at Irene Ma's two hotel restaurants. I worked seven days a week, sometimes for thirteen hours a day. Still, I felt like I had spare time. Occasionally, when I talk about this time in my life, someone will say, "That's crazy!" or "When did you sleep?" I try not to roll my eyes when I hear that—I had no choice. This is just what an immigrant has to do to make it. Honestly, I don't understand people who talk about being busy with one full-time job. Let's do the math here: I was working eighty hours or more per week. Lisa wasn't there, so she wasn't a distraction. I didn't really have any hobbies, or a lot of friends, and I wasn't taking any summer courses. The town was small—in a car you could get from one end to the other in seven minutes—so if I had to be at the kitchen at 7:00 a.m. for the breakfast shift, I could leave the house at 6:45 a.m. and still arrive with plenty of time to spare. I ate at work, so I didn't have to think about feeding myself. Because it was labor, I didn't bring any stress home. I worked the shift and then I was done. So, after sleeping and showering, I had time to go to the movies, go for a swim, or go for a run.

Come fall, Irene kindly bought me a return ticket to UBC, a very nice gesture since the cost of the flight was a lot for me. Even though I worked eighty hours a week all summer, I still didn't have enough to cover school. I took out loans that would take me a few years to pay off.

***

A couple years after Lisa had arrived in New York, back in Vietnam her mom had had a stroke, leaving her confined to a wheelchair. Just a few months after that, she and Lisa's two sisters finally had their interviews with immigration in Vietnam and were approved to move to the United States. They'd been waiting ten years, and then it happened, with what felt like no warning. Lisa had just a few months before they'd be arriving at her doorstep in Brooklyn. She was beyond ecstatic, but she was also worried—it was all happening so fast, and she didn't feel ready for the responsibility of caring for three more people in addition to her brother. When she got sick, it took her a total of three hours to go to the doctor, whose office was a long subway ride away from her apartment. The idea of getting her mother the care she needed—and negotiating the subway with her wheelchair—seemed daunting, if not impossible.

Lisa took some vacation time and flew to Seattle, where a friend from Vietnam lived. She saw that the city was pretty and peaceful and close to Vancouver (and UBC), and I'd like to think that she decided to move here not only because it made sense for her family, but because she wanted to be closer to me.

A friend in Seattle tried to dissuade her: "It's hard enough to get settled in one place," she said. "Why would you want to start all over again? Finish your degree, then think about it. What about your job at the nonprofit? Jobs like that don't grow on trees." Her supervisor, Michael, was the only one who encouraged her, saying, "Lisa, you gambled your life to be here. If you had the guts to escape Vietnam and survive in New York, you can survive anywhere."

So, she uprooted herself yet again and flew across the country to take up residence in a two-bedroom apartment in Seattle's Beacon Hill neighborhood. It cost more than her apartment in New York, but she wanted her family to feel comfortable when they arrived. To that end, she bought some furniture she couldn't afford, putting a sofa, a dining room table, a couple mattresses, and a TV on her credit card. Career-wise, her friends had been right: social work jobs did not, in fact, grow on trees, and soon she learned that a master's degree was required for any job beyond entry level. Lisa moved to Seattle in May, and her family arrived at the beginning of August. After paying the airfare for them to come, she did not have much savings left. She had to accept a job at the kitchen of a deli in Uwajimaya, a local Asian grocery store. Later she found another job at a local travel agency, and then she got a better paying job at Northwest Airlines. Finally she started working as an insurance agent for MetLife. Her brother managed to get a job at McDonald's, and then he got a position in the meat department at Uwajimaya. Lisa was thrilled to be reunited with her family, but she missed her old job and friends, and felt overwhelmed with caring for her mom and introducing her sisters to their new country.

***

We did the long-distance thing for about a year. My love for Lisa grew; at the same time, I saw how much she was struggling, and I was wracked with guilt that she may have moved, in part, for me. What if she'd stayed in New York and kept her social work job? It broke my heart to see her working at a grocery store when she could have been a social worker. And I was still in school, always just on the verge of being broke and unable to support her, at least financially. Her family needed more help than I could provide, and even though I loved her, I knew she'd probably be better off with someone else. She needed someone who could pay the rent, buy the groceries, be there for the day-to-day in the ways that she needed, maybe even buy her something pretty every once in a while. What if I was never able to give her the life that she wanted, the life that she deserved?

On one visit in particular, Lisa cried as she told me about what she was dealing with. Her brother was depressed and moody, still resentful. Sometimes he did not want to go to work, so it continually fell to Lisa to make enough to pay the rent for everyone. She had managed everything and anything, but I was worried that she might break from the pressure. I was so busy with work and school that even though everything I did was done with her in mind, I felt like it wasn't enough.

So, I decided that I would do her a favor: I would end it. That would give her the chance to find someone more established who could take better care of her and her siblings and her mom.

So, one weekend, I met Lisa in Vancouver. I still have a photo from that visit. In it, Lisa and I are sitting together, and we are not smiling.

On my way to meet her, I practiced what I would say: *You are too good for me. I can't give you what you need. I love you. You deserve better.*

I can't remember my exact words, but I said what I believed, and what was the exact opposite of what I really wanted. I took her hands, warm and small in mine, and looked into her eyes. By the end of it, we both were crying.

I walked her to the bus station and hugged her one last time. "Forget me," I said. "Be happy." She didn't say anything, just looked into my eyes before turning away. I watched as she walked away with her head down, something I'd never seen her do. Through the window, I could see her making her way down the aisle to take her seat. Her pretty oval face appeared in the window, two tears running down her cheeks but her chin held high. I could feel the tears on my own cheeks—I hadn't cried when my grandmother beat me, or when my dad had gone missing, or even when I had been tortured. But I was crying now. *This is the end,* I thought, *the last time we'll ever see each other.* More tears filled my eyes, and I blinked, trying but failing to stop them from falling. We held each other's gaze through the window as the engine started and the bus pulled away.

For the next year, I kept myself busy, doing everything I could to keep my mind occupied. Later I learned that Lisa had done the same. She had to work incredibly hard to support her family, and because she felt like she needed to be strong, she hid her sadness and pretended like nothing had happened. I also found out, later, that while we'd been broken up, many men had pursued her, and she'd dated around and tried to forget me, just like I'd told her to. Meanwhile, I was way too focused on studying to be interested in any of the many nice girls at UBC, or at least that was what I told myself. I didn't date at all, in fact. Maybe it was because school took up all my time and energy. Or maybe it was because I was too deeply in love with Lisa to think about anyone else.

We didn't talk for that entire year. No phone calls, no letters, nothing. My heart hurt that whole time, but I held in my sadness as best I could. *It's the right thing,* I tried to convince myself over and over. *She's free to make a better life.*

Lisa, meanwhile, was working hard and trying to forget about me. Later, she'd admit that almost a year into our breakup, she'd called Anh, a friend and colleague from Lutheran Immigrant Refugee Service in New York, and told her the situation. Anh listened patiently, then told Lisa a story about her own sister, who had sacrificed a good marriage to take care of her family. "I have a good family now," Anh said. "But my sister is still single. She lives with me and my family. Don't make that same sacrifice.

Because of her, I get to have a life, but it's unfair that she does not. This is America, Lisa. You need to pursue your own happiness."

That was probably just what Lisa needed to hear. Then she talked to Katie, another good friend and Chinese Vietnamese refugee who'd arrived ten years earlier and had seen the many ways that refugee relationships survived, or fell apart.

"You still miss him," Katie said. "When I look at you, it's so easy to see that you're miserable. If you still love him, then go to him."

***

It was Valentine's Day of 1993, and Lisa was coming to British Columbia to see me and some other refugee friends. I was nervous to see her again—maybe she'd see me and decide that she'd made a mistake in calling me, that I was just this skinny, broke guy with nothing to offer her, and that I would never be what she needed me to be. I wouldn't have blamed her if she felt that way, since this was, in my insecure moments, what I wondered about myself. All I knew was that I'd missed her terribly, and I felt sure that I'd made a mistake in letting her go.

We met on Granville Island, a bustling public market in Vancouver surrounded on three sides by False Creek. The day was overcast and cold, but the rain that had been pouring for what seemed like forever had momentarily paused. The summer venues, the water park and the kayak rentals, were closed. I didn't have any money to spend, but I was still excited to walk around the market area with my friends.

The first time I saw her after our long separation, my heart sank. Our time apart hadn't blunted my feelings for her in the slightest. *Dammit,* I thought. She hadn't changed a bit, except that she was even more beautiful than I remembered. With the last of my cash, I bought her a bouquet of flowers. It was pointless to fight it: I knew that I couldn't live without her.

"You are the only one for me," I told her.

"And you are the only one for me," she replied.

That night, when our friends had all gone home, I asked her to marry me.

CHAPTER 10

Math Tutors Wanted

The bulletin caught my eye from halfway down the hall. I was in the middle of my third year at college, walking down the hall of the math department. MATH TUTORS WANTED, it read. I pulled one of the tabs with the phone number and called BrainChild Education Center in Richmond, a city within the metro area of Vancouver. That phone call completely changed my life.

The next day, I took two buses to get to the education center before office hours for an interview and a math-tutor qualification test. Mary, one of the managers of the franchise, greeted me at the door. She seemed to be a nice young woman, quiet, soft-spoken, and courteous. She led me into the carpeted classroom, and I was immediately impressed by the rows of gleaming white tables and the line of bulky computers along one wall. I felt comfortable in her presence right away, and that put me at ease during the test. After I finished, I sat silently across from her desk while she graded it. It took a lot of concentration for me not to fidget or pace around the room. After a while—what was probably only a few minutes but felt like hours—Mary put down her pen and said, "Congratulations, you've passed," and offered me a job.

I immediately called Lisa in Seattle. "I'll be making eight dollars an hour!" I told her excitedly. Again, I was easily impressed when it came to money.

My first day of work at BrainChild was a few days later, on a Friday, in the spring of 1993. After the one-hour bus ride, I showed up to find the place packed with tons of elementary and middle school students. At the entrance, there were two storage shelves lined with baskets of manila folders labelled with the students' names. I was excited and confident: since I already had so much experience tutoring, I knew it wouldn't take me long to learn the drill. As I taught the students, I was thoroughly impressed by what I was seeing in front of me. I was naive about business expenses, overhead, and that sort of thing, but I could do basic arithmetic. I thought: *BrainChild charges each student $50 per month. Going by all those manila folders, let's say they have roughly one thousand students a month. That equals $50,000 a month gross income. They pay me $8 an hour. . . .*

I couldn't wait to finish work that day. As soon as I could, I rushed back to my dorm room and, as usual, called Lisa. "Their business is so great! They must make so much money!" I practically shouted into the phone. "I love to teach *and* I love to do business! So, this is the perfect combination!"

Then I hung up and called my manager, Mary.

"Mary," I said, cutting to the chase, "I'm quitting." There was a moment of what I assumed was shocked silence.

"You don't like your job?" she finally said.

"I love it."

"Then why are you quitting?"

"I want to do what you're doing. Please, show me how," I said, leaving out what I was thinking: *I smell opportunity.*

Mary laughed, then cleared her throat. She was probably thinking, *This young man is ridiculous.*

"Seriously?" she said. "You really want to learn this business?"

"Yes, I do."

"OK, then why don't you come back next week and talk to my husband, Edmond?"

After that, I never returned to work as a tutor at BrainChild. I never even picked up my paycheck for that one day of work. I was too busy learning the ropes from Edmond. He and Mary had purchased the license from BrainChild. Weltson, the licensor in Toronto, had spent a lot of time refining it in practice. They told me that if I wanted to do this, I had to buy the license from BrainChild and start my own center. My business skills were rusty. I hadn't used them since running my recycling operation in Vietnam. But I was eager to put them back to work.

During that time, I was disappointed to discover that the Vancouver tutoring market was fully saturated, and if I wanted a viable business, I'd have to open a tutoring center elsewhere. I still had a year left of college, which would give me some time to plot and plan.

***

On September 11, 1993, seven months after I'd asked her, Lisa and I got married.

We were mismatched in a lot of ways, at least in the traditional sense, and both of our families couldn't help but voice their reservations. People say that no one is ever good enough for their daughter and, for Lisa's family, this was definitely true, at least when it came to *me* as her husband. They'd known me since I was a little kid, had seen me fighting in the streets or stealing fruit from the back of a truck. Or worse. I'm sure they thought that, what with Lisa being so educated and refined, her potential husband should be at least her equal. One of her sisters even said to her, "You are my hero. I look up to you, and so I expect a lot from you. You're so smart, so educated! Why would you want to marry someone like Hao?" I agreed wholeheartedly that she deserved better. I was working on the education piece, but becoming more refined was perhaps beyond my capabilities.

My family, meanwhile, didn't want me to marry a girl who was older than I was, although you'd never have known that by looking at her. One of my uncles said, "C'mon, you're in college! There must be so many pretty young girls at UBC. Why would you want to marry someone older? Take your time, date around. Be young and enjoy yourself!" My grandmother, the family matriarch, wasn't too keen on the marriage, and my parents suggested that we wait until after I'd graduated college, likely hoping that our passion would cool by then. Only Aunt Binh and Uncle Nam, who had heard all about Lisa and my feelings for her during the time that I lived with them, supported us.

It was easy for me to shrug off their disapproval. I've never been one to care much about what other people think, and I believed that we'd waited long enough. In most areas of my life, once I make a decision, it's hard to convince me otherwise, and this was no exception. Lisa is the same way, so eventually our families gave in, though not without a fair amount of resistance. Still, their approval meant a lot, especially to Lisa. Her family was—and is—so important to her, and she would do anything to make them happy.

She and I agreed that marriage would give us peace of mind, and that was the most important thing. No more moving, no more back-and-forth, no more uncertainty. Traditionally, in Asian families, marriage vows are final—divorce is not an option. This was comforting to us, but not so much to our parents.

I wanted to be married, but I did not want a wedding. As had been the case forever, I didn't have any money, and I was too proud to ask for help from my relatives, especially given that they'd been against the marriage in the first place. Lisa's family didn't have any money, either. To avoid going into even more debt, I suggested that we have a simple, courthouse-style wedding, but Lisa hoped that throwing a big party for our relatives would help to soften them, make them happier and more accepting. She was the eldest daughter, after all, and I was the eldest son. I could understand her reasoning, but that didn't make the whole thing any less impractical. Still, I agreed to it—Lisa, determined to fulfill her duty as the eldest daughter and win back the respect she'd lost when she'd decided to marry me, was set on throwing a party worthy of her mother. My parents were still too newly arrived in Canada to legally leave the country, so Lisa and her family would have to come north for the wedding. To save money, we decided to have the ceremony in the common area of my dorm and host the party at a nice restaurant in Vancouver. For months, Lisa drove up on the weekends, and, with the help of my distant aunt Chau, found a photographer and bridal gown, booked some rooms in a motel for family, and made a reservation at Kirin Restaurant for the party. Meanwhile, Lisa worked full-time during the week and did her best to deal with the stress of supporting her disapproving family. With all that weight on her small shoulders, something had to give.

Later she told me that her mind had been full, that she hadn't been paying attention when she ran through that red light. She'd just been driving along, tallying, checking off, organizing in her head, staving off the sadness that overtook her whenever she thought about our family's resistance. And then, deep in thought about place settings and bridal bouquets, she felt a violent jolt, and all that noise in her mind went silent.

Thankfully, the car accident left Lisa with only a few bumps and bruises, a sore neck, and a scratch or two. The car, however, was completely totaled, and emotionally the accident left a mark, too, not just on her but on her family. Lisa was too frightened to drive for almost a month, and the close call rattled the rest of them free of some of their stubbornness. An accident like that makes people rethink themselves and their relationships—what if they'd lost her? What if their last conversation had been bitter, all about why she shouldn't marry the person she loved?

Finally, they signed on wholeheartedly. To her they said, "We are no longer opposed. Do whatever you want—as long as you're happy, we support you."

***

The traditions of a Chinese wedding are a little different from those of an American one. In the morning, the groom comes to the bride's house and serves tea to his future in-laws, then takes the bride with him to his house, where she does the same for her future in-laws. Since our housing situation was a little less than traditional, Lisa's family was staying at the motel she had booked in Vancouver. At least our families would be riding in style: Lisa's boss, Clement, had volunteered to chauffeur us around in his Mercedes.

Before we could do that, however, I had to get past Lisa's bridesmaids, who were guarding her that morning in her parents' motel room. According to tradition, I had to go negotiate for my bride, and they would push to get the best bargain. There are legends of determined grooms forcing open the door and physically pushing their way through, but luckily it didn't come to that. I can't remember what obstacles they put in my way, or exactly how many Canadian dollars in multiples of nine—an important number for weddings, nine being a synonym for "forever" in Mandarin—I had to pay to win my bride. Either way, I happily overcame all obstacles, refused to feel any sense of embarrassment in front of our well-dressed family and friends who were watching from outside the hotel room, and paid what they asked.

It wasn't raining that day, but, from the room to the car, Lisa's sister-in-law held a red umbrella above the bride, to protect her from the evil eye. Sitting in the back of the Mercedes, we were chauffeured to Queen Elizabeth Park to take pictures. We had no idea that this lush 130 acres of arboretum and gardens was such a hot spot for wedding photos—we were among probably thirty other couples. It was gorgeous—the leaves were just beginning their autumn transformation, and the green grass and purple flowers next to the Japanese maples' reds, oranges, and yellows provided a colorful contrast to the neutral tones of our clothing. Lisa wore a white satin gown with a long train and puffy sleeves, and around her neck she'd draped a necklace of pearls. Her veil had lace flowers sewn in, the white highlighting the black glossiness of her hair. Her lipstick was a beautiful shade of red. I wore a gray suit with a white shirt, a red bow tie, a red cummerbund, and a red handkerchief tucked in the breast pocket. Red is a lucky color. I think we looked pretty snazzy.

Then it was time for the tea ceremony. According to custom, Lisa changed out of her bridal gown into a Chinese traditional red silk robe, which she'd borrowed from Aunt Chau, who'd brought it all the way from Hong Kong for her own wedding two years earlier. We held the ceremony in my dorm, where red paper cutouts of the Chinese double happiness symbol had been hung around the room, adding some color to the beige, industrial carpeting and furniture. Heaps of oranges, candies, teas, and flowers had been piled on the kitchen table as a gift for the ancestors.

Usually, when the bride or the groom kneels down and serves the tea, the parents give a red envelope with lucky money and say, "We wish you to be together forever. Take care of each other." Everything went smoothly at Lisa's place, but when it was Lisa's turn, my mother said, "You take good care of Hao." This was, in essence, a withholding of her blessing. I was furious, but I did not want to cause a scene or disrupt the process, so I bit my tongue. From the way that Lisa bowed her head, I could tell that she'd noticed the insult, too. *I will take good care of her,* I vowed to myself. *We will be together forever.*

Lisa and I had overcome our families' resistance. I'd paid the price. Our parents had drunk the tea. Lisa and I had survived war and poverty, a week at sea, a year in a refugee camp, so much time apart, and now, finally, we were married.

Roughly one hundred fifty people attended the reception, the majority being my relatives. We'd reserved fifteen tables at Kirin Restaurant. Lisa's side of our now-joined families occupied four tables, while folks from my side took up the other eleven. The banquet hall was decorated in the reds and golds that, to the Chinese, symbolize joy and good luck, and the Chinese lanterns cast a warm glow over the faces of our guests. I'd changed into a rented black tuxedo, and Lisa had changed into her third outfit, a simple silky dress in a light peach color, with a big bow across the chest. The reception wasn't like Western-style wedding banquets, in which there are appetizers followed by the main course, and then dessert. This was the traditional ten-course feast, with every kind of food you can think of: lobster and deep-fried prawn balls; fish maw, dried scallop, and shredded chicken soup; marinated chicken in abalone sauce, noodles stewed with mushrooms and tender scallions; and more—I can't remember it all. Everything smelled delicious; I do remember that. Lisa and I, however, were so busy talking to everyone, being congratulated, and saying thank you that we hardly had a moment to take a breath, let alone eat. Still, I'm pretty sure I managed to get at least one bite of the towering, four-tiered wedding cake.

Everyone seemed to be enjoying themselves, if you can judge that based on the conversation volume and the speed at which the food disappeared. Even though I hadn't wanted a big wedding, I was glad that Lisa got her way—it was so much fun, and it seemed like our families were starting to loosen up. I tried my best to hold off stewing over the bill that was coming—there'd be plenty of time to worry about that later.

At the end of the party, after most of the guests had left and the dishes had been cleared, a waiter brought the bill in its black leather folder. "Whenever you're ready," he said, setting it down next to me on the white tablecloth. Lisa and I looked at each other. All that hard work had paid off, and there we were, after all we'd been through, finally married, finally free and able to imagine a tomorrow and all the tomorrows after that during which we'd be together. For a second, I looked at her and remembered how she'd looked on the boat—her face burned by the sun, her hair tangled and stiff with salt, her dirty clothes hanging off her bones, the fear and exhaustion in her eyes. And now she was radiant, her face flushed, her dark hair healthy and smooth, her dress perfectly clinging to her slender frame. She was the most beautiful bride in the world.

I checked the bill, and then handed it to Lisa, who looked it over carefully before putting it back down on the table. We gathered all the red envelopes and stacked them in a pile.

"Don't worry," I said to my new wife. "We'll be fine."

One by one we tore open those red envelopes. The cash went in a stack on the table, which I eyed as it grew taller and taller. When all the red envelopes had been rifled through, Lisa counted the cash. I waited.

It wasn't quite enough. I looked over at my mom, who was sitting with my dad and grandma at one of the recently emptied banquet tables. She'd been watching this whole time, and when she saw me look over, she got up.

"I see," she said, walking over. "Now I have to pay." I could sense Lisa blushing beside me; I could feel her body tense. My wife hated to ask for help—she always liked to be the one helping. But in this one instance, she'd just have to bite the bullet and accept my family's aid, however ungraciously it was given.

Of course, we couldn't afford a honeymoon. However, during Christmas the following year, we traveled to France and the Netherlands on Northwest Airlines, using the free tickets Lisa had access to as a company employee. In France, we stayed at Lisa's friend's house, and in the Netherlands, we stayed at my aunt Lien's home. During the latter visit, we mentioned our plan of opening a tutoring school after I earned my degree the following April. She offered us a loan to get us started. Now, I hoped, I'd be able to provide for Lisa, to build something that would give her the safety and comfort she deserved.

CHAPTER 11

From Refugee to Immigrant

Oddly enough to us, our magical wedding did not solve all our problems. To be honest, the time after was pretty rough. I was still in school and poor, and we still lived apart. I'd informed the university that I'd gotten married, so the housing department moved me into a suite in a low-rise dorm, more appropriate for married students. Lisa drove up often to stay with me. We both had to balance a heavy workload, and we each struggled in our separate ways. *I just need to graduate,* I thought to myself, *and then at least we can struggle together.*

In 1994, Kitty bought me a yellow 1979 Nissan King Cab pickup truck. That was my third car—the first was a $500 Dodge that I learned to drive on, selling it for $450 after a year of use. The second one had a stick shift, and I sold that one before going to college, because parking was too expensive. This last one cost Kitty a few grand, which was a lot of money back then, especially because she was a college student working part-time to try to save up some money. She bought it so that I could visit Lisa, so at least one more member of my family approved of our marriage. Once I had my pickup truck, my routine changed. During the week, I studied super hard, and right after school on Friday, I'd take a nap to avoid rush hour traffic before driving down to Seattle. The car was old and without a tape player, so I bought a portable one to review the class lectures I'd recorded.

My graduation commencement took place on a bright day in April of 1995. Unlike my high school graduation, this ceremony was not very exciting. There were no special awards of recognition, no fancy calculators. Instead, I was one among thousands, and the thing I remember most is the long wait while one by one everyone walked up to the stage for their diploma. Still, it was a very important event—I was the first of my entire family to get a college degree. Lisa was there, and I remember her tears of joy.

I'd barely flipped my tassel before I was on my way to Seattle. In the past few years, I'd probably crossed the Canadian-US border a hundred times, but that day, since I'd be relocating permanently, the border agent stopped me so that he could inspect my pickup truck. It took roughly four minutes to go through my two suitcases and two milk crates filled with books.

"You have one year to return and collect the rest of your stuff," he said.

"Thanks, Officer, but I won't need to come back. This is all I own," I said, rolling up the window. When I left Vietnam to go to the Philippines, I had nothing. When I left the Philippines to go to Canada, I had nothing. When I left Canada to go to the United States, I had a little bit more than nothing—student loans. I no longer felt like a refugee—I was now an immigrant.

***

Lisa had scrimped and saved and borrowed money from her sisters in order to come up with a down payment for a house for her family, located on Vashon Avenue in Renton. Linh, the sister who was with me during the escape attempt when I'd almost been shot, had put in roughly half the money for the down payment, but it was under Lisa's name, and Lisa would pay Linh back. This was the best way to avoid family conflict, it was agreed. And later, Lisa could return the favor and loan money to Linh if she needed it.

This was in July of 1994, less than a year after our big wedding. If you asked Lisa how she managed to put on a wedding and make headway into real estate in such a short amount of time, she would probably say something like, *I was very frugal.* In 1989, she'd arrived in the United States with nothing but the clothes on her back. Over the course of five years, she'd managed to save enough money to buy a split-level house with a yard and a two-story garage. Her sisters each had a room to themselves on the main floor, and her mom had her own bedroom one level up, next to the master bedroom Lisa and I would be sharing.

I moved in with them on a sunny spring day, and it didn't take long for me to unpack. After our years of living countries apart, her face was now the first thing I'd see in the morning and the last thing I'd see at night. Finally, I was home.

My new wife supported me while I struggled to set up a BrainChild Education Center. I'd signed a license agreement with Mary and Edmond and agreed to pay a 40 percent royalty on monthly growth. To put that in perspective, today I charge a 12 percent royalty for Best in Class Education Center franchisees. I hadn't thought about money because I loved what I did, and obviously I had no idea what the term "profit" meant. Thank goodness for Lisa.

Lisa: You pay forty percent. How are you going to make money?

Me: What do you mean? We get to keep sixty percent!

I didn't listen to her. How naive I was! I was just so passionate about teaching and running a business. I was thinking more along the lines of, *Can we affor٠ the loss? What is the worst-case scenario?* I was so young and I thought that, if the business failed, I'd get a job, repay the debt to Aunt Lien, and then start all over again. Since I had little to lose, I took the leap without fully looking, though Lisa's tried her best to get me to take a more cautious approach. I hadn't factored in the reality that the BrainChild franchises in British Columbia had a huge established market, and that, with our tiny list of students, 40 percent would soon lead us to bankruptcy. Again, I was good at math, but not so much at business. Still, if I hadn't signed on with BrainChild, I wouldn't be where I am today.

Though I'd driven through town on the way to Lisa's many times, Seattle was still a foreign land to me. Lisa knew the area well, and so, after she got off work, she'd go with me and a real estate agent to scope out locations for our franchise. She was the one with all the connections, and again much of the burden fell on her. Let this be a lesson to you: if you are good at everything, people may just ask you for everything! Most of the time, my wife doesn't seem to mind—in fact, she really loves to take care of people as much as she can. That's just who she is.

Then she became pregnant. We were thrilled, scared, excited, all the things that a young couple might feel when faced with all the changes that a baby would bring. Late into the night, once

I'd returned from work, Lisa and I would talk about the future, the idea of which I was starting to love more and more. We were going to be a family, our own little unit in this great big world.

Then, just as I was starting to get used to the idea of our having a baby, Lisa suffered a miscarriage. These days people talk openly about this common occurrence—it really is something that happens to a lot of women. At the time, I was very uninformed, and it came as a shock and a disappointment. It wasn't easy on Lisa, emotionally or physically. She needed to take some time off to recover, and she managed to stay home and do nothing despite that not really being her sort of thing—Lisa had never been one to sit around eating bonbons and watching soap operas. I tried to be there for her, and at the same time I had to keep up with work. I did my best to take care of Lisa during that time, but I didn't know what do, what would make her feel better. I just wanted her to be OK.

***

We opened the first location of BrainChild Education Center in June of 1995, in downtown Bellevue. At that first center, I did everything—I was the math teacher, the paper grader, the receptionist, the janitor. (Yes, I even swept the floors and scrubbed the toilet.) We'd hired one other instructor to teach the English classes, but in the beginning, we had hardly enough students to keep her occupied, let alone paid. After covering the rent, I certainly wasn't getting any kind of compensation for my work. This is the nature of starting a new business—it takes a while to get it off the ground. During that time, we really depended on Lisa's paycheck from her job as a reservation agent.

The work was hard, and the days were long and filled with uncertainty. Lisa got pregnant again, and miscarried again. I'd had no idea how bad a miscarriage could be, how painful and debilitating. She had to take more time off work, but she'd used up all her sick leave and had to take two weeks off without pay. There we were, without any income whatsoever. Thankfully, Lisa's two sisters were able to cover the mortgage.

This was a turning point for me. I hadn't come all this way in life to let my wife down, to not be able to make ends meet. In Vietnam, I'd always been able to make money, but back then, I also wasn't as concerned about playing by the rules. So once Lisa was feeling up to it, she and I went to Vancouver to see Mary and Edmond.

After briefly catching up, I laid out our situation. "Look," I said, "I have no income, and we are not making any money. I know that we signed an agreement to pay forty percent, but we just can't make that work."

Mary and Edmond looked at each other but didn't say anything.

"OK, so we charge students fifty dollars a month and pay you forty percent of that," Lisa said. "What if we raised the fee to sixty dollars a month and paid you eighteen dollars of that, which is thirty percent? That's only two dollars less than what you've been getting, and this would help us get on our feet."

Mary and Edmond were not unsympathetic to our situation, and they agreed to call the licensor, Weltson, in Toronto. After a few minutes of discussion on the phone, they agreed. We were very happy with the new arrangement. We implemented these changes, and slowly we started to pay the rent and pay the other teacher, with a little bit left over for me to pay myself.

After seven or eight months, I opened a new office in Seattle, at the Asian Resource Center in Chinatown. I rented a classroom there two days a week—a weekday and a weekend—and hired another teacher. I was working from 4:00 p.m. to 8:00 p.m. weekdays, and I began to look for another job in hopes that this could help to supplement my scant income and give us a little more breathing room. It was a slog, and there were plenty of times when I'd go through the want ads while the clock ticked away. As I filled out application after application, I had to face the fact that a math degree was not as valuable professionally as I'd hoped. Truth be told, I could not get a job to save my life, not even a minimum-wage substitute-teaching gig.

This turned out to be a blessing in disguise. Had I gotten another job, I wouldn't have been able to put 100 percent into growing my business at this vital moment. If the pay had been good enough, I might have even let go of BrainChild altogether. But since that wasn't happening, I had no choice but to develop the fledgling business. Slowly but surely, business picked up. I wasn't making much—well, hardly anything—but I loved what I did. And, more important, Lisa believed in me. So, I kept going, and every so often, a new student or two would arrive at my doorstep. Business in the Bellevue center was picking up, and soon we outgrew the tiny classroom in the Asian Resource Center, and I moved the Seattle location to a different spot in the heart of Chinatown. In a redbrick office building next to Ho Ho Seafood Restaurant on Maynard Avenue and Weller Street, the eighteen-hundred-square-foot classroom space felt like a sprawling campus.

There was a good reason that I was working so hard: Lisa was pregnant again.

CHAPTER 12

Navigating Parenthood

I watched with awe that year as Lisa's belly went from bump to beach ball. The pregnancy was very complicated, and she had to quit her job at Northwest Airlines so that she could stay home on bed rest and get ready for delivery. She had all the worst side effects of pregnancy—vomiting, swollen feet, gestational diabetes, high blood pressure, severe flu, and, lastly, depression. Finally, on a beautiful spring morning in 1997, our beautiful baby boy, Louis, was born.

It took two days for Lisa to deliver. On top of that, the anesthesiologist had somehow messed up not one but two epidurals—Lisa felt the pain the entire time. At a certain point, Lisa's doctor decided to call in a specialist—I don't know what his job title was, but he was an expert in more difficult deliveries. The new doc decided that enough was enough and, after taking firm hold of the clamps, pulled the baby out. Our baby had a conehead.

"What kind of creature is this?" I said, mostly joking, upon first seeing him.

"Don't worry," my mother-in-law said. "You just have to massage his head every day. It'll be fine."

Thankfully, she was right, and baby Louis's head rounded out after ten days of gentle massage. It was so easy to fall in love with this quiet creature—Louis was an easy baby, and extremely cute, with a sunny disposition. My sisters-in-law both worked at medical clinics, and they told us that, of the thousands of kids they'd seen, no one was like him. He was always happy, always smiling.

Those days of Louis's infancy were full of joy. Lisa and I couldn't get over how beautiful he was, how good-natured and smart. He grew and grew and grew like a weed, filling out into the ideal chubby baby. There'd be no hunger for this American-born baby, no thought to where the next meal was coming from or who'd get the biggest helping of sauce. I'd make sure of it.

While Lisa was home taking care of our son, I was working hard at BrainChild, pushing where I could to develop the business. It wasn't easy or predictable, and I worried each month about what my pay might be. Even though I was still basically buying a job, I wasn't actively looking for something else. But, without Lisa's income to rely on and with another person depending on me, I was definitely open to whatever might come along.

A year after Louis was born, Michelle, the mom of an eighth grader, came in and asked to see me. I assumed there was some kind of problem, that her daughter's grades weren't improving, or that she just wasn't getting it. But instead of complaining, Michelle said, "I really like you. You've helped my daughter tremendously with math, and for that I'm grateful."

"Thank you," I said, relaxing. "That is wonderful to hear."

"It's the truth. You know, I'm an instructor at Renton Technical College. And I'd like you to come teach with me."

So, an opportunity fell in my lap, and what did I do? I hesitated. This would be my first job in the United States, a real job with real structure and responsibility and pay. More worrisome, it would come with a real boss, someone whose rules I'd have to follow. It'd been a long time since I'd followed someone else's lead, and for those of you who know me, that's not exactly my strong suit. I mulled this possibility over in my mind, weighing the pros and the cons. Rules? Con. Not being the boss? Con. Stability? Pro. Steady paycheck? Pro. Getting to teach math? Pro. Being able to support my blossoming family? Pro.

I applied for the job. Michelle was my reference, and, because she'd put in a good word, I was hired to teach in the adult basic education department. I worked on a team with her and two other instructors, Deanna and Barbara. Since I was there, I decided that I might as well take some of those more practical classes that I'd missed out on at the University of British Columbia. All of a sudden, those formerly empty daytime hours were filled to capacity: I taught at RTC and at two BrainChild locations while also going to school full-time to get a degree in computer science and programming. Seven days a week I was busy studying or teaching, breathing math and computers, and sleeping when I could. I practically started dreaming in code!

My hours were long and varied, so I hired nannies on and off to help Lisa so that she could manage one of the tutoring centers. Every day I'd come home to learn of some new development, like the time that one of Lisa's friends asked her whether Louis knew the alphabet yet. He was only two years old! But, being Lisa, she went out and bought him an alphabet puzzle, and by the time I got home that afternoon, he could do it by himself. From that moment, he was into reading, and he read anything he could get his hands on.

Louis started preschool when he was three years old. He had an excellent teacher, Ms. Vicky. We adored her—with her, it wasn't just playtime. She was always teaching the kids something, whether it was the days of the week or the different kinds of weather. At the end of the school year, Lisa went to the parent-teacher conference, and Ms. Vicky told her that, unfortunately, she wouldn't be able to move Louis up to the four-year-old group because he wasn't where he needed to be, academically speaking. Apparently, he did not know all the letters of the alphabet.

When Lisa told me that, I laughed. "What is she talking about?" I asked her. "Are you kidding me?" Well, soon enough it came out that, because everything was so easy for Louis, he'd been pretending not to know his ABCs just to play a trick on his teacher! A three-year-old—can you imagine? At the time, not only could he recognize all the letters; he was even able to read children's books! This would be the first time that Louis demonstrated how he could be too smart for his own good, but it certainly wouldn't be the last.

***

To be honest, we'd originally planned to have only one kid, but Louis was such a good boy, and we thought that maybe he was lonely. By 1998, our BrainChild locations were bringing in real income, as was my teaching job. We were able to pay off my student and business loans, but we'd been able to buy a bigger, nicer house in Renton, still close to that first one, where Linh and her husband still lived. Neither Lisa nor I is superstitious, but we truly believed that Louis had brought us good luck. That year was a very happy year, with lots of successes to celebrate. In 1999, Lisa's sister Linh got married, as did my sister, Kitty. We didn't have to struggle so much anymore, and from that moment, it felt like the stormy days were over. So, we decided that it was time to have a second kid.

Albert was born in October of 2000. This time, Lisa's pregnancy was the total opposite of the previous one. Everything went so smoothly that she'd felt perfectly capable of working more than full-time at BrainChild in Seattle during the summer.

Lisa and Kitty were both pregnant at the same time, with due dates for their babies within the same week. Albert, however, had different plans. Maybe it was the stress of working so hard, twelve hours a day, seven days a week, while taking care of a toddler in the evenings. In any case, Lisa was only seven months along when our second son decided to enter the scene.

I'd driven over from our Bellevue location to the Seattle location to pick up Lisa. We were planning to go to a friend's party. She was working at the computer when I arrived. Seeing me enter the office, she turned off the computer and stood up. Suddenly, she was screaming.

"Oh my god! I . . . I think my water just broke." She rushed into the restroom. "Hao," she called. "I'm bleeding . . . a lot."

"Hold on," I said, trying not to show panic in my voice. "I'm calling Dr. Graham." He told me to take Lisa to the emergency room, right away.

I led Lisa out to the car and drove her to Overlake Hospital in Bellevue. Every so often, I glanced over at my wife. She was breathing steadily but shallowly, her head leaning back against the seat and her eyes closed. *Please,* I prayed. *Please.*

At the hospital, she was immediately whisked off to a room. I paced the tile floor in front of the reception desk, waiting for news. The nurses eyed me sympathetically but had no information to give me. I clenched my teeth to stop myself from asking the only questions that mattered: *Is my wife OK? Is the baby OK? Are we going to lose the baby? Am I going to lose them both?*

Finally, a nurse came out and told me that Lisa was fine, the baby was fine, and they were just going to keep her there until they could get her stabilized. I hadn't noticed that I'd been holding my breath, but my big sigh of relief alerted me to the fact. *OK,* I thought. *They're OK.* I felt even more relieved when they allowed me in to see her. Looking small and frail in her hospital gown, Lisa was sitting up in the bed when I entered the room. The fluorescent lighting emphasized the grayish tone of her skin, but she at least had the strength to give me a smile. She patted the bed beside her. I sat down, careful not to jostle her. "Don't worry," she said, then patted her belly. "I heard the baby's heartbeat. Everything's all right. But they told me that I have to be on bed rest until the due date." I was so, so relieved, but I knew that she'd have a really hard time doing nothing for the next two and half months.

Two days later, I was at Renton Technical College when I got a phone call from a nurse, who told me that I could pick up my wife at three o'clock. The past couple days, Louis had been crankier than usual, crying and whining and asking where she was. I could hardly blame him—I was anxious, too, wondering when she'd be released. Now, finally, she'd be coming home.

Normally I'm punctual to a fault, early the majority of the time. But this time, fate decided that I was going to be late. This was incredibly lucky: that lateness probably saved both Lisa's and Albert's lives.

The reason I was running behind was that I'd gone to Chinatown to buy some ingredients for soup, thinking that I could make Lisa something warm and nutritious for her homecoming. I'd quickly loaded up my basket with green onions, fresh ginger root, sesame oil, a head of cabbage, chicken, and pork liver, which the Chinese believe helps to build up the blood. Since Lisa did most of the cooking, I wasn't sure what we already had in stock, so, just in case, I bought a little of everything. With time to spare, I made the purchase and loaded the grocery bags in the car. Everything was smooth sailing, until I pulled onto the highway.

Though nothing from that time can compare to today's Seattle gridlock, on the way to Overlake in Bellevue, I ran into some traffic, causing me to arrive forty-five minutes late. I cursed under my breath as I rode the elevator up to the childbirth center. *Of all the days to be late*, I thought.

Just as the elevator doors opened with a ding, I heard a voice calling for doctor assistance over the PA system and saw a light blinking red and nurses running into Lisa's room. Later they told me that she'd taken a shower and was getting dressed to go home when she started bleeding heavily again. I didn't know the details, but that last part was obvious the moment I walked into her room—there was so much blood, on the floor, on the bed, that for a second I was almost certain she and the baby hadn't made it.

"What's happening?" I yelled as people in scrubs rushed around me. "What is happening to my wife?"

A nurse put her hand on my shoulder and began to steer me toward the waiting room. "I'm sorry, sir, but you're going to have to wait out here. We'll come and get you as soon as we can."

I've been through a lot in my life, including real, blood-on-the-floor torture. I've nearly drowned, died of thirst, been shot. But I have to say that there is no greater torture than waiting helplessly while someone you love beyond words is bleeding somewhere you can't reach and may be dying along with your unborn son. *That* is the worst torture I've ever lived through.

As I paced under the fluorescent lights, between the beige chairs, table, and carpet, every second felt like a century. I called my aunt Binh in Prince Rupert.

"It's OK, Hao, shh, shh. Take a deep breath. It's OK. They have everything under control. Lisa's one of the strongest women I know. She'll be all right," she said over and over to try to calm me down. I listened to her while down on one knee. I didn't even have the strength to stand. I felt like screaming, like tearing apart every piece of furniture in the room with my bare hands. I was devastated: I didn't know whether my baby and my wife were going to live or die. I thought about Lisa's previous miscarriages and felt a cold chill run down my spine. *What will Louis and I do without them?* I wondered.

I don't know how much time I spent out in the waiting room, but it felt like a lifetime. Our obstetrician, Dr. Graham, was not available at that very critical moment. His partner, Dr. Rogers, had filled in for him. Finally, he came out to the waiting room.

"We've done a C-section," he said. "An ambulance from Children's Hospital is on its way. Some nurses will take the baby—they are better equipped to help him there."

"Is Lisa OK? The baby? Can I see them?" I asked.

"You can see your wife for just a moment. But she's lost a lot of blood and needs to rest."

Once they'd rolled Lisa into a room, I went in and, for a moment, stood in the doorway, just watching her. She was so pale, as if all the color had been drained out of her, which it had. Her black hair looked even darker against her ashen skin. But then I saw her take a breath and thought, with immense gratitude, *She's alive.*

Very late that night, I went to Children's Hospital to see our newborn son. There he was, under the hard-plastic dome of the incubator, this itty-bitty thing barely longer than the palm of my hand. He weighed just three pounds, five ounces. He was skinny, dark, and very long like *youtiao*, a Chinese donut. Tubes stuck out from all over his little body, and his chest was concave because his lungs hadn't had a chance to fully develop. I cried that first time I saw him. He was so skinny. The nurse handed him to me, and I held him as gently as I could, careful not to crush this fragile creature. He didn't look like what you'd expect a baby to look like. He was not chubby or rosy, with open, unfocused eyes. Instead, he was covered in bandages and had half a dozen tubes sticking out of his body. His eyes stayed closed.

"Talk to him. He can hear you. Let him know you are here," the nurse said.

I swallowed the lump that had gathered in my throat. "I am here, Son," I said. "Be strong. Mama's waiting for you."

The next few days, I traveled between Lisa and baby Albert, from Overlake to Children's and back again, to pick up Lisa's breast milk and deliver it to him. The nurses gave Albert just a little bit at a time—1 cc, 2 cc. I'd watch them poke him several times a day to test his red blood cell count and check for anemia. They put him on caffeine to manage the apnea, and if he stopped breathing for too long, the breathing machine would beep. "He's doing much better," I'd report to Lisa, who'd had a blood transfusion after hemorrhaging so much. "Getting bigger and stronger all the time."

After several days, Albert was transferred back to Overlake Hospital to be with his mother.

Lisa was shocked when she first saw him. I wasn't there, but she called me, crying. When I picked up the phone, all I could hear was her weeping and saying, "Baby . . . baby . . . the baby . . ."

"Lisa," I said over and over, trying not to panic. "What's happened to the baby?" Finally, once she'd calmed down, she told me that, when the nurse had handed him to her, she hadn't dared take him.

"I feel so bad and so guilty," she said between sobs. "He is so tiny and so vulnerable. But I felt him when he was inside—he was very healthy and strong! I must have worked too hard and did not take good care of him."

Lisa was released from the hospital after a week. But they gave her a room in the hospital for another week so that she could be with Albert. He spent the first sixty days of his life in an incubator. This was when our family saying became "Are we gonna die?" Albert and Lisa truly did almost die, and I'd had to face what it might be like without them. To me, there could be nothing worse in this whole world than losing my family. By comparison, everything else in life is no big deal. Lisa and I use the phrase all the time these days, whenever there's a problem or a challenge or someone's getting frustrated about something. "Are we gonna die?" one of us will ask the other. "No," the other will be forced to say. "Then, what's the problem?"

***

I often think about how the different births and early years of my children's lives may have affected the way we raised them. Louis was such an easy child, so well-mannered and clever, and perhaps because of this, I treated him more harshly, allowed him less room for mistakes. Albert, on the other hand, had given me and his mom such a scare that all I really cared about was that he was healthy. I was more lenient with him, less strict. He was underweight and hyperactive as a baby and child—he couldn't sit in a car seat with a seat belt on for fifteen minutes. Any longer than that and he'd kick his feet and scream as though we were murdering him. But when confronted with real pain, he never cried, even when he fell off the jungle gym or crashed his tricycle or did any of the million things kids do to test their limits (and stress their parents out). The only evidence of injury was the big blue bruises that would show up on his body later—I wonder if, because of all the poking and prodding he'd undergone during his first couple months, he'd somehow developed an immunity to pain.

When Albert turned two, Lisa said, "Before, I did not know what 'terrible twos' meant. Now, I do." Albert bent all the window blinds, pushed over the living room chairs, turned on the stove and the kitchen faucet, and tipped the hot water out of the kettle, all within five minutes. He drew on the walls. One day, our babysitter called Lisa in a panic and told her that Albert had decided to water the TV. The TV had made a big noise and then went black. Later, when I asked him why he did that, he said that he thought the TV was thirsty, just like him. We rarely took him out, because every time we went to a restaurant, he misbehaved. One moment, he was on the table; another moment, he was under the chairs. One time at a Chinese restaurant, he climbed up on a chair and turned off all the lights.

"As long as he's healthy," I'd say to Lisa after a day of his bouncing off the walls had pushed her to the brink. In a way, I didn't have any expectations for Albert, not because I didn't think he was capable, but because I was simply grateful for his being alive. But from Louis I expected everything.

On Louis's first day of kindergarten, while lining up to go inside, he'd been able to read all the signs. He was always ahead of the class, easily bored, and prone to distraction. When he was in second or third grade, I took him in for the gifted test. In the car afterward, he shrugged and said, "That was easy." This turned out to be the standard mode of operation going forward—Louis was smart, sometimes too smart, and he could ace a test without trying. This meant that he saw no point in doing homework. Why would he? Since he could successfully wing it every time, he never learned to slow down, study, or get organized like the rest of us. I can remember when he was in twelfth grade, and I asked him what his final grades were. "Dad," he said, "it's a combination of letters." (At least he inherited my sense of humor.) Getting him to actually turn in his homework became a constant battle. There were just too many (pointless, in his opinion) steps:

1. Remember the assignment.
2. Do the assignment.
3. Print out the assignment.
4. Put the assignment in backpack.
5. Bring backpack to school.
6. Remove the assignment from backpack.
7. Turn the assignment in to teacher.

I'd see him spending all weekend on a project, only to hear from his teacher later, asking why he hadn't done it. "He did do it!" I'd say, knowing that at that very moment it was probably sitting in the bottom of his backpack, or on his desk, or in his locker, or even in the printer at home. Unless I turned it in, it just wouldn't get there, and what was I going to do—go to school with him every day? Not possible. Over and over, the same thing happened, and neither of us would ever learn his lesson. If you've ever tried to get a kid to do something that he just doesn't think matters, you know exactly what I'm talking about. And here I was, an educator, and I couldn't even get my own son to turn in his homework!

It was very stressful for me, and I ended up trying to monitor Louis's life, which of course led to conflict. Looking back, I can admit that I was too hard on my firstborn. Mostly I did what I believed was for his own good, but a part of it was about protecting my own reputation and my own livelihood. There was no way to separate the two. But I wish I'd had the awareness to sit myself down, take a deep breath, and have an inner dialogue along the lines of:

Are we gonna die?
No.
Then what's the problem?
You're right—he's not on drugs, he's not in a gang, he doesn't get in fistfights, he doesn't ride his motorcycle drunk. He was even a National Merit semifinalist.
Exactly. And remember, Hao, you were way worse.

I wish that I'd cut Louis more slack. And I wish I'd let him fail more often. That may sound strange, but I just couldn't let go of control enough to let him figure out the way on his own. In fact, he's said as much. His senior year, he and the Mercer Island High School marching band were scheduled to play at the Seahawks halftime show. This was a huge opportunity for a kid, right?

The night before, I asked him if he needed me to wake him up. "Nope," he said.

In the morning, he rushed in. "Dad! I overslept. The bus to Safeco Field is already gone. And my bass trombone is locked up inside the school!"

So, what did I do? I volunteered to drive him to school so that he could pick up his gear. This was a Sunday, and the school was locked. We pounded on the door and shouted, hoping that someone—a custodian, a teacher grading papers, anyone—would hear us and let us in. Instead, the alarm went off and security arrived. *Thank goodness,* I thought when the men in blue approached. *They'll let us in.*

"We're here to turn off the alarm, and that's it," one of them said. Believe it or not, another boy from the band showed up. His mom happened to have a direct line to one of the teachers, whom she called. She woke him up—this was early on a Sunday, after all. I'm guessing that most overworked and underpaid teachers prize this weekend morning for catching up on sleep, and boy, do they deserve it! Still, he came and unlocked the door for us, and Louis rushed in to grab his gear. We barely made it to the game in time.

"Dad," Louis said to me afterward, "if you hadn't done all that, I probably would've learned a hard lesson." He knew that failure was an option, but I didn't. If he was hungry, I fed him rather than letting him figure out how to feed himself. I wish that every now and then I'd let him go hungry, let him get a bad grade. Because then perhaps he would've learned something and felt freer to make a better choice next time. Perhaps I could have spared us many fights, and our relationship today would be in better shape. Or not. We'll never know, because I always pushed him, and he always pushed back.

I think that Albert became attuned to this tension between us very early on. This may have been what gave him such intense drive and self-control—I never ever had to worry about him turning in his homework on time. He was self-correcting to the highest degree, practically killing himself to get the best grades. An A- was never good enough, and if he didn't get that A, he'd get so mad at himself that I couldn't bear to get mad at him, too. My boys switched places as they got older—where I'd never had to worry about baby Louis, kid Louis and teenager Louis caused me no end of grief. And where I'd worried for every moment of Albert's early years, kid Albert and teenager Albert were every parent's dream.

I don't want to say too much more about my sons, because I want to respect their privacy. I'm telling you this much not only because there is nothing more important or motivating in my life than my sons, but because through them, it's easy to see that the world works in mysterious ways. You could call it karma—after the hell I put my own parents through, after embarrassing my own mother by refusing to go to school, there's a little bit of cosmic justice to the way my relationship with Louis developed. Really, if you look at it, he's just like me—clever, manipulative, stubborn, and allergic to authority. No wonder we butt heads. Albert is like me, too, of course—he's hardworking and charismatic, goal oriented, and able to navigate whatever system he finds himself in. In them, I see Lisa's brains and her sensitivity. Beyond that, they are their own people, full of their own surprises and quirks.

***

I'm not a person who lives in the past. I've done a lot of bad things in my life—I stole, I fought, I lied and manipulated. I disrespected my parents. If there's one thing I regret, though, it's my parenting. I was so busy with work all the time, and I had no one to guide me. If I could go back, I would take parenting classes and spend more time with my family. I'd take more time to just enjoy them. I would have been gentler and less demanding, more patient, more curious about my sons' points of view and feelings, more invested in seeing my children as individuals with unique talents and intelligence. I wouldn't have nagged or yelled. I would have taken the time to pause and notice that the life I'd fantasized about in Vietnam had in fact materialized, that we had enough to eat and a safe place to sleep and that no one was going to knock on the door in the middle of the night.

It's so much easier to see the missteps in retrospect. We're all just winging it, after all. My first priority was work, and there's nothing I can do to change that fact now. And here I am, with a successful business, and hopefully enough time to learn from my mistakes and improve the relationships I have with my family. And Louis did graduate from high school, though he managed to give me a million heart attacks along the way. He tested both me and Lisa at every step, and so, at graduation, we felt almost like it was a dream, considering how close he came to not getting his diploma. I'll tell his kids someday what he put me through, and maybe he'll get his own just deserts. For now, he's at my alma mater, UBC, majoring in music.

I love my boys, even when we don't get along. Even when we want to kill each other! I think this is a common way for a father to feel, and I'd guess that many kids feel the same way about their parents. But I hope that they know how much I wish for their happiness, and how much I love them.

CHAPTER 13

Are We Gonna Die?

Most people like a success story. It's nice to read about someone making it to the top of the mountain and to imagine ourselves there, in their shoes, with the wind in our hair, the hard work long behind us.

But failure is what makes that story interesting, and real. Who cares if that mountain climber made it to the top if every step was easy and predictable? That's boring. The compelling parts of the story are all the wrong turns, twisted ankles, and avalanches. That's what makes the success worthwhile, and worth reading about. I've failed many, many times, and that's not something I'm ashamed to admit. I brag about my failure! Because failure has made me who I am today.

In 2001, I left Renton Technical College for a job at Microsoft as a contractor. It wasn't without regret—I loved teaching, but I thought that this new job would lead to bigger things. When a developer had a problem, they'd call a hotline and, on the other end, I or another of the developer support staff would answer. We'd troubleshoot, talk through processes, that kind of thing, and quickly I was promoted to full-time, trading in the orange badge of contractor for the blue badge of employee. Lisa, meanwhile, was working full-time, raising the children, and managing our home and two education centers.

This was during the first tech boom, when everyone dreamed of becoming a millionaire overnight. Like everyone else, I wanted to get a ton of stock and retire early and sit on a big fat bank account for the rest of my days. *This,* I decided, was the ticket to a more-than-decent living, not BrainChild, which was still just barely surviving.

I enjoyed the prestige of working for one of the giants of the industry, but pretty soon it became clear I wasn't cut out for talking on the phone all day, or any task involving that kind of structure or, well, a certain degree of monotony. I was tied to my chair and my phone, and I only talked to developers who were in the middle of a crisis. Finding solutions to problems could be satisfying, but dealing with stressed-out or frustrated people all day, every day, started to wear on me.

And, to add insult to injury, I wasn't getting rich quick. I woke up one morning thinking, *Something is missing.* When I told my boss, John, this, he said, "You're great, Hao. I think you should stay on, see what happens. You have a future here." I'd learned a lot, but I disagreed—I just couldn't envision doing it forever. Then, one day, Lisa sat me down for a serious conversation. She said, "Hao, I am so tired. I need your help. You need to devote more time to our business and family." A lot of people thought I was crazy, but that conversation pushed me to do what I already knew I wanted to do: leave Microsoft.

Even though I now believe that doing too many things at once is a waste of time, back then I was still searching, hoping for a stability that I still wasn't sure BrainChild could provide. BrainChild was still a back-burner project, and I quit Microsoft with the idea that I'd be on to my next adventure soon.

A couple of weeks after I left Microsoft, one of Louis's friends from preschool was having a party at Chuck E. Cheese's. While the kids were bouncing off the walls in a postpizza frenzy, I got to talking to a couple of the other parents, Julia and Nathan Chan. Julia was a loan officer, and Nathan, coincidentally, had also recently quit a job at Microsoft. He also had a mortgage broker license and was planning on opening a mortgage company. When he heard that I'd just quit Microsoft and that I taught math, he tried to recruit me as his loan officer. Over breadsticks, he explained to me how the mortgage industry worked. My antenna went up. *I smell opportunity,* I thought.

"Let's do it together," I said. "You have the license; I'll run the business."

As soon as I got home from the party, I called my good friend and CPA, Andy Yeung. We have a lot in common, and we're still friends to this day. One of the things that originally brought us together was that we both have a strong entrepreneurial spirit. "Andy, I have a crazy idea," I said, cutting to the chase. "I just met a guy who has a mortgage broker license. Why don't we join up with him, rent a space, recruit a bunch of loan officers . . . and start making some money?"

Within two months, we'd found a thousand-square-foot space in Bellevue. This was June of 2002. I didn't do the mortgage sales—I was in charge of training, compliance, and, as one of the owners, making sure that we had the best team possible. Not long afterward, I asked Kitty to join the company. She'd majored in accounting at UBC, and once she'd come on to help out, we were able to recruit close to fifty loan officers.

It seemed only natural to then get involved in selling and investing in real estate. Two sides of the same coin, right? Once you start investing, it's a slippery slope—you just want to keep investing, and you're always looking for the next big thing. The mortgage business led to the real estate business, which led to the restaurant business, which I knew nothing about. But I was—still am—always game to learn something new. If this sounds like I was moving really fast, that's because I was. That's how I operated—always on to the next thing!

And through Andy, in early 2003, I just happened to meet the owners of a five-hundred-seat Chinese buffet restaurant in Renton who were looking to sell some shares. It was already up and running, it was profitable, so I thought, *Why not?* Once I'd bought in, I joined the biweekly meetings at the restaurant after the doors had closed for the night. Over frosty bottles of Tsingtao and steaming plates of pork lo mein and sweet and sour chicken, we'd talk shop. Inevitably, someone would observe that Chinese food in Seattle was nothing compared to that in Richmond and Vancouver.

"Hey," I said one day, "why don't we open a *good* Asian fusion restaurant in Seattle?"

Several months later, Purple Dot Café was born. Andy was also one of the partners. You see how fast the two of us make things happen when we are motivated? Lisa, the voice of reason, tried to slow me down. She has a strong entrepreneurial spirit, too, so it wasn't that she was opposed in theory—the problem was the impulsive decisions and sloppy, unconsidered execution. But no matter how much sense she was making, her words fell on deaf ears. Like I've said, I'm stubborn, and once I commit to something, I don't stop until I see things through. What could she do? She was stuck—if she convinced me to forgo the investment and the restaurant ended up being successful, I'd resent her for the rest of our lives. I suppose she could've left me, but besides having children and a home together, we really loved each other. We'd been through so much together already, so she wasn't going to quit on me now. Finally, after much futile discussion, she gave me the go-ahead. She would have to let me try this crazy thing—and she'd have to let me fail.

In Chinese, the name "Purple Dot Café" means something like "The Hangout Place," and we made sure that it was the hippest spot in the heart of the International District. The ceiling we painted black, the walls eggplant purple with a thick band of silver rolling through the walls' center like a belt. We hung a few red lanterns above the red, neon-green, and black chairs and booths, creating a contrast with the bright blue, pinks, whites, and tropical greens of the aquarium. All of this was super cool at the time. We also hired a very talented and trendy interior designer named Sanny, from Vancouver. We scouted out the best chefs from Vancouver and developed an incredible and huge menu that, we hoped, would be appealing to everyone from the picky five-year-old to the eighty-five-year-old grandma with more traditional tastes. To that end, we divided the menu into three sections, the first offering food in the traditional Hong Kong style, simple fare like wonton noodle soup and congee. The second was more American-influenced for the American-born kids, with fries, steaks on sizzling plates, ham omelets, and clam chowder. The third had a long list of wok- and hot-pot-inspired creations such as Szechuan-style black pepper chicken and mapo tofu, aimed at dinnertime and family gatherings. Then there was the separate and extensive drink menu, with all kinds of teas, coffee, and exotic fruit juices and smoothies.

We thought we were being smart by covering all the bases, but it turned out to be a disaster. The labor costs were super steep—we had to hire three lines of chefs to handle the three parts of the menu, plus the large waitstaff. On top of that, we undercharged for good quality and lots of quantity, hoping to attract everyone with a stomach, even those on a budget. I didn't know that in business it's best to find a niche and cater to it, rather than try to make everyone happy all the time. Still, for months after opening day, there was a line out the door. Everyone wanted to eat at the new hip spot and was willing to wait for more than an hour to do so. The other restaurateurs in the International District were pissed—they felt that we were stealing their business.

You'd think, based on that initial surge of interest, that we'd be set. But on paper it didn't work out that way—we continued to bring in revenue, but not enough to keep up with our high costs. We had a lot of customer turnover each day, but we were not profitable.

"It's OK," we said to one another at the investors' meetings. "Let's keep going. We'll just fix things as we go."

Then, at one of these meetings, someone had an idea: "Why don't we open another one?" We were all so motivated—and so clueless!—that we managed to pressure one another into making the next move before the previous move was complete. We were overconfident, sure that we could make a profit because, we figured, we were already so busy. Some of the investment partners and I opened two more restaurants, one in Burnaby, British Columbia, and one in Las Vegas. Not long after that, I sold my shares at the Chinese buffet in Renton because I needed the cash.

With these three locations, there was always a fire to put out. And putting out fires required money.

In short, we had no idea what we were doing. This is where our failure came in, in a *big* way. I'm the first to admit now how naive and unprepared we were. The truth is, we opened those restaurants simply because we *wanted* to open them. We didn't know the business, and that quickly became clear. We didn't charge our customers enough for their meals, we didn't create a good team, and we underestimated labor costs. We didn't take the time to figure out protocols and put systems in place as we grew. Some of the investors were willing to put in more capital as needed and others weren't, and we hadn't established a strict partnership agreement to deal with that discrepancy, making it impossible to enforce equal investment.

We were hemorrhaging money from the get-go. But oh, how much fun I had, at least in the beginning. I loved the restaurant business. Every morning, I'd pop out of bed, excited to face the day and all the ups and downs it would bring. I thrived on meeting the chaos head-on, learning something new every time something went wrong, the rush I got when the kitchen was busy and the dining room was full. Sure, I could've made it easier on myself by planning a little more thoroughly and waiting for the first restaurant to make a profit before opening the second. But who needs preparation and patience when you've got chutzpah?

***

It was July Fourth 2003, and we were at Lisa's sister Linh's house for a barbecue. Twenty or so of us were perched on lawn chairs in the shade on the yellowing grass, sipping frosty beers and watching the kids run through the sprinkler. Linh's husband, Alan, was manning the grill and Lisa and her sisters were talking, laughing, and sipping their drinks when my phone rang. My caller ID said it was Janie, a good friend who lived nearby.

"Hello," I said. "What's up?"

"Hi," she said. "Just calling to double-check that you're coming to our barbecue soon." We'd been planning on leaving in the next hour or so to go to Janie's mom's house for this second party.

"Yup," I said. "We'll be there soon."

"Great. Oh, and by the way, I saw smoke coming from your neighborhood."

"OK," I said, thinking nothing of it. "Probably just a bunch of teenagers with some firecrackers."

"Yup. Just thought you'd want to know."

After thanking her, I hung up and bit into a tasty chicken wing. The barbecue sauce was sweet with a little bit of kick to it, and the meat was that perfect combination of salt, protein, and fat. Lisa had seen me on the phone and was walking over.

"Who was that, calling on a holiday?" she asked, sitting down in the lawn chair next to me.

"Just Janie calling about the barbecue," I told her. "She said something about smoke in our neighborhood, too." I took another bite of chicken.

Lisa jumped to her feet. "What? There's a fire in our neighborhood, and you're eating wings?"

"C'mon," I said. "What are the odds that it has anything to do with us? Probably a bunch of kids horsing around."

"Let's get out of here," she said, and began waving to get the boys' and the nanny's attention. I shrugged and stood up.

"Got to go," I told Linh and Alan as I reluctantly walked out.

The driver's seat was hot and nearly burned the backs of my arms as I sat down. The nanny buckled in the kids in the back, and

Lisa buckled her seat belt in the passenger seat. The drive took about five minutes, and from a distance we could see the smoke drifting, spreading out across the neighborhood. I couldn't tell where it was coming from, but as we got closer, my heart started to race. It seemed like it was coming from our block. I suddenly had a horrible feeling that it was, in fact, coming from our house.

Multiple fire trucks and police cars were blocking the road, and a news helicopter noisily circled overhead. I pulled up as close as I could and parked with a jerk. The boys were crying, scared of the big crowd, the firefighters and police, and the smoke. "Stay here," I said to the nanny. "Please, stay with the boys."

Lisa and I threw open the car doors and got out. "Ma'am, sir?" said an officer standing behind the police barrier. He held up his hands, palms facing us. "You can't go this way."

"That's our house!" Lisa said.

"Let us in," I said. All I could see was smoke and the great streams of water coming from the firefighters' hoses.

This was the second house we'd owned in Renton, the one we'd purchased in 1998. It was big, more than three thousand square feet, with large windows facing the sidewalk and a three-car garage. The boys had grown up in this house. The family room was packed with their Legos and books, all the things little boys needed to be happy in this world. I'd always wanted a house with a ton of skylights. I loved the idea of waking up in the morning and checking the weather just by looking up. I loved to watch the rain fall against the glass, and the way that the natural light came down to light up the room. Well, I got my skylights that day. When the fire had finally been put out and it was deemed safe to go in, I looked up and saw that above me was *all* skylight! The roof had been fully torched, and the smell of burned plastic, wet drywall, and smoke was overwhelming.

Later we'd learn what had happened: witnesses told the police that they'd seen fireworks land on the roof. (Apparently no one saw where they'd come from, or so all the neighbors claimed.) The roof was made of shingles, and, in the July heat, they must have been as dry as matchsticks. A neighbor had seen the smoke and immediately fetched our garden hose, but the roof was too high to reach, so he'd called 911. In the seven minutes it took for the fire trucks to arrive, smoke had turned to fire, and then it was just too late.

The water had soaked into the drywall holding up the second floor, causing it to collapse. Eighty percent of our home was destroyed by either the fire or the water. All our clothing, beds, furniture, and the curtains Lisa had so thoughtfully picked out had gone up in flames. Our dishes, the carpet, the kids' books and toys, everything. Fortunately, one closet on the bottom floor had survived, along with the photo albums and other odds and ends stored inside. And, in another turn of good luck, I'd brought my laptop to the barbecue in order to show my family some photos of our most recent vacation.

For most folks, this would have been an absolute catastrophe. Our adjuster told us that fires like this one often lead to divorce—the stress of putting a home back together can just be too much for some couples. But Lisa and I were pretty calm about the whole thing. Our kids were safe; we were safe. "Are we gonna die?" we asked one another later that evening. We'd had nothing before, and we'd survived. We'd survive this, too.

Around this same time, my parents agreed to move from Prince Rupert to Vancouver, BC, a roughly three-hour drive from Seattle. Lisa is very traditional in terms of Chinese custom, and she believes that taking care of the older generation is a duty, not a choice. For years, she'd been trying to convince my parents to retire, but their strong work ethic had prevented them. Finally they were convinced, and we helped them purchase a house in Richmond, a city that many considered to be a "little Hong Kong" in Canada. It just so happened that, when I had the chance to fulfill a filial duty by buying my parents a house in a Chinese community, our own house burned down. One of life's little ironies.

***

The fire did not kill us, but it did set us back a bit. But we did not have to start from ground zero, fortunately. Unlike in the past, we had more than just the clothes on our backs—we had bank accounts, a large support system, American citizenship, thriving children, and a stable, extended family.

We rented an apartment near Purple Dot Café, so that we could eat all our meals at the restaurant. Lisa got busy cleaning up the mess the fire had made while also taking care of Albert and Louis and managing the Bellevue and Seattle locations of BrainChild. Our lives were very, very full.

My family was good. My house was gone. My businesses were . . . not great. OK, they were failing.

It's easy to see in hindsight where I went wrong, but, at the time, it was really hard to step back and take a look around. Today, I could walk into a hotel or restaurant, and, in fifteen minutes, form a decent assessment of how they're doing. But while I was investing in restaurants, I was happily blind, which eventually led to some real problems. What had once been jolly and optimistic investor meetings soon became shouting matches, with everyone pointing the finger at everyone else. What had been exciting and unpredictable soon became stressful and unmanageable.

Don't forget, I was also running a real estate business, a mortgage loan business, and two education centers. People would call me while I was in the middle of tutoring math with questions about getting a loan. People would call me at the restaurant to inquire about signing up for an English class. People would call me at the loan office to talk about a capital commitment for the restaurant. I took every call, stepping away from whatever I was doing in order to attend to something else. I had no priorities, no direction, operating in panic mode 24-7. I was busy, busy, busy, but without a vision or a mission. No wonder nothing was growing—I was like a chicken with its head cut off, multitasking and spreading my energy among so many things that nothing could actually get done. Well, saying that *nothing* was growing isn't exactly true. One thing definitely was growing—my belly.

I like to say that it took a lot of hard work and dedication to get such a big belly. A lot of money, energy, and food went into the making of it, a lot of investor breakfasts and new-client brunches and business lunches and dinner meetings and after-dinner drinks. All that eating left little time for exercising. Add to that the stress, the long days, and the sleepless nights, and not just my weight but my health as a whole started to suffer.

One by one, the restaurants went out of business. In Las Vegas and Burnaby, we simply told the staff not to show up for work the next day, then turned off the lights and locked the door behind us. We pretty much gave away the Seattle location—at that point we were losing so much money that if we got even one dollar from the person who took over the lease, that'd be a gain.

Then the housing bubble burst. Home sales went down; foreclosure rates skyrocketed. After already being drained by the failed restaurant ventures, I had nothing left to see me and the company through this crisis. So, I shut down the mortgage company, sending the fifty or so loan officers out into the world with only my best wishes. My real estate business went dormant. And that was that.

It's easy to talk about failure after years have passed and things have turned around. At the time, however, the way things fell apart was very painful for me. I should have listened to Lisa, I told myself. I should have slowed down and thought things through. Usually when I don't listen to her, things eventually go south. I spent many nights awake, going over and over all the ways things went wrong, all the ways I'd screwed up. I'd lost some good friends in the process, and I agonized over that, too. To top all that off, I was unhealthy, stressed, exhausted, and over-weight. It was very hard on me and the family, both financially and emotionally. I was completely drained, utterly depleted. But still I was optimistic, because that's just who I am. A new opportunity would present itself, I felt sure of it.

CHAPTER 14

A New Vision

This catastrophe pushed us into the next chapter of our lives. Before the fire, Lisa and I had been talking about moving to Bellevue so that we could enroll the boys in Somerset Elementary. I suppose the fire was the nudge that we needed—we bought a house in Bellevue, and then moved back to Renton once the house had been rebuilt. Soon thereafter, we decided to move to Mercer Island, where we live to this day. Years passed, our boys got bigger and smarter and more set in their personalities. I got more experienced and, as luck and failure would have it, more dedicated to my true calling.

In 2010, my phone rang early one morning. It was still dark and quiet outside, too early even for birds to be singing. It was Weltson, the owner of BrainChild, calling at what was, to him in Toronto, a reasonable hour.

"Hello, Weltson," I said, rubbing the sleep out of my eyes. I cleared my throat. "Good morning! What's up?"

"I'm ready to retire," he told me. "I want to sell the business. But before I put it on the market, I thought I'd ask you first—would you consider buying me out?"

That woke me up better than a cup of coffee ever could. I'd long dreamed of owning the business, or more specifically, having more control over the business and its expansion. Over the fifteen years that we'd worked together, I'd put forward all kinds of ideas to Weltson, only to have most of them shot down. He was a more conservative businessperson than I am, and he was happy to stay stable rather than grow. Because I was only a licensee, my hands had been tied—without his approval I couldn't do a thing.

Now, finally, opportunity was knocking on my door, a chance to take what Weltson had started and run with it in the direction I wanted.

After hanging up the phone with Weltson, I called Edmond. He and I were still something of a team, and I always valued his opinion. He was the one who'd gotten me started, after all. My investment failures had made me a little more cautious and, to be honest, I was scared to take on such a big project by myself. What if, after plotting, planning, and dreaming for so long, I finally had the chance to manage the business my way and then ran it into the ground? As in the past, Edmond had my back. He agreed—we'd go in on this together.

After a few weeks of negotiation, Edmond and I bought BrainChild. Sadly, Weltson passed away a few months later. Eventually, Edmond and I changed the name from BrainChild Education Center to what it is today: Best in Class Education Center.

The idea of being at the helm of the franchising operation had been stewing in the back of my mind for a long time. Of course, theory is easier than action, and everything is easier said than done. I refused to make the same mistakes I had in the past, so I set about getting to know as many elements of franchising as I could. I had a lot to learn.

Creating and selling franchises is a much different animal from running individual tutoring centers. I won't get too technical here, but you need a lot of things I hadn't thought of, like an operations manual, a website, marketing tools, and a franchise disclosure document. And you need money, which I didn't have much of after buying the business from Weltson. But I was willing to risk everything, to put every penny I had into this dream. What was that risk compared to getting on a boat going to destinations unknown without food and water, or moving sight unseen to a foreign country?

Naively, I expected the phones to be ringing off the hook the moment I'd taken the helm. That's not exactly how business works—you can't just hang your shingle and wait for the customers to arrive. I didn't know that you have to spend a lot of time, energy, and, of course, money to bring in franchise leads, not to mention the blood, sweat, and tears it takes to close a deal.

Soon it became apparent, however, that Edmond and I weren't exactly on the same page. While I wanted to put everything into growth, with the idea that sacrificing our present income meant a bigger and better future, he wanted to put only a certain percent of our profit aside for investing in the growth of the franchise operation.

I think that this difference in leadership philosophies impacted our growth—or lack thereof—for those first two years. He wanted to grow slowly and steadily, much like Weltson had done; I wanted to grow aggressively and go all out—that is my style. This caused a lot of tension, a lot of disagreements that we had to work through every step of the way. We were very busy dealing with this interpersonal element, and that took time and energy away from figuring out franchising. In fact, we only sold a few franchises during that time.

Now, it's easy to see how all my business failures were life lessons for me, and that ultimately all roads lead to Rome. True, I lost money and time. But I learned a lot, including the fact that, unless I die, there's always another chance to get it right.

On a more practical level, the real estate business provided me with the knowledge that would inform my choices down the road. I can help my franchisees with site selection, letters of intent, lease negotiations, and loan applications. It also taught me about patience, a trait that is definitely *not* in my blood; I learned that there is no such thing as overnight success. Every business is an investment; everything takes time. Even when you think you've hit a peak, there's no way to know if tomorrow will bring another rise or the beginning of a fall. But the business journey is so much fun—if you can handle the stress.

I also learned that if you're doing five projects at once, you can only give each project 20 percent of your energy. That may seem obvious, but it's really not, at least not while you're doing it. I learned this the hard way.

I think that this also taught me a lot about passion. If mortgage brokering or food service were really, truly my passion, then I would have stayed with it. I'm not a quitter, and roadblocks won't stop me if I'm determined to get somewhere. The fact that I gave up shows that neither industry was right for me.

In the middle of 2012, Edmond and I decided to go our separate ways. The split was not easy, but it was amicable. He was a very important person in my life, a mentor, and he and I will always be friends.

Once I'd bought his shares, I became the sole owner of the tutoring business. Now it was fully mine, and I could run how and where I wanted. I could give 100 percent to one project, and let the other projects go. In a sense, I was finally ready to gamble, to go for the big jackpot without having any kind of backup plan or safety net. It was all or nothing.

It took me almost two decades to have this realization: real progress can only be made through that 100 percent—100 percent passion, 100 percent dedication, 100 percent effort, and, most important, 100 percent focus.

***

Since then, Best in Class Education Center has expanded into more than fifty franchises across the country, from the Pacific Northwest to Florida, New Jersey to California to Texas. I love franchising for a number of reasons. First, it allows me to meet some of the many people who share my passion for both education and entrepreneurship. Second, it allows me to help those aspiring entrepreneurs to become people who can then contribute to their communities by creating new jobs for teachers and positively impacting the lives of students and their parents.

Priya Venkat is one such franchisee. I met her more than ten years ago. She'd moved to Seattle from India in 1997 and started working as a researcher at the University of Washington. After eight years at UW Medical Center, she transitioned from research to clinical work. She also started a family.

Priya and I initially met because she was concerned about the local school system and was looking for a way to help her own kids in math. Her older child was four years old when he started at Best in Class, and, over time, Priya and I began to have more conversations about the center's mission and education in general. We discovered that our enthusiasms aligned, and when she moved to Dallas in 2013, I helped her set up a business of her own. Now she has twenty-three employees and two centers, and she's hoping to eventually expand further.

Kevin Lee is another franchisee whom I've known for more than ten years now. He moved to the United States in the late 1990s as an international student at the University of California, Berkeley. While in school studying applied math and statistics, he began tutoring math at a BrainChild center located in Oakland (in addition to working in the restaurant industry and at the post office). He really liked the flexibility of the curriculum and how he and his fellow tutors were able to tailor it to suit each individual student's needs. After graduation, he contacted me to talk about opening an education center of his own in San Francisco's Chinatown, where many new Chinese immigrants were looking for a way to help their kids integrate into and succeed in school. I was overjoyed to help him set it up.

Now, on Saturdays and Sundays, he runs his business, and on weekdays, he works at his full-time real estate property management job. That's another thing he likes about franchising—he has the flexibility to create his own schedule, so he can operate the education center on his terms.

At the end of the day, education is not big business, but for people who love it, it can provide both a sense of fulfillment and a decent living. Nothing makes me happier than seeing my franchises succeed. In the same vein, franchisees tell me that nothing makes *them* happier than seeing their employees and students succeed.

***

All this growth did not happen overnight, and it required the help of many people. In 2014, I joined Entrepreneurs' Organization (EO), a global network of entrepreneurs interested in growing their business and bouncing ideas off like-minded people. I thought that I'd get some good advice on how to grow a business there, but I've received so much more than that. Without a doubt, EO has helped me grow my business—but, more important, it's helped me grow as a person, improve my relationships with family and friends, and open my eyes to the world. I've learned how to better take care of family, community, business, and self. The people I've met in EO are my people, my tribe, and part of what we do together is share everything—our ups and downs, our hopes and dreams, what it really takes to run a business and to live a life at the same time.

Through EO, I met Ron Huntington, a business coach who's become a close friend and a mentor. He's helped Best in Class Education Center become what it is today by working to develop our core values: positivity, energy and passion, adaptability, collaboration, and efficiency. I also met my other mentor, Ted Tanase, who deserves a lot of credit. He helps me stay focused on the big picture. He introduced me to Sue McNab, who mentors me and a couple of my team members.

In the past few years, I've attended several EO Universities, EO Alchemy, the EO Executive Masters Program, and the Global Leadership Conference. These are all great learning opportunities for me to grow as a business leader and as a person. Whenever I hear a good speaker, I see whether he or she has a book, and, if so, I buy it. Think about the return on investment: you spend only twenty dollars or so, and you get a window into a person's experience, all the mistakes they've made, and life lessons they've learned. Now I read at least two of this kind of book a month.

My executive team, my internal staff, and all our many center managers and teachers keep the business running day to day. Bauhinia, the office manager, started as a student when we first opened, as a second or third grader, with her younger brother, Sunny. They were first generation, the children of immigrants from Hong Kong who'd moved to Seattle and opened Bamboo Garden, a vegetarian and kosher-certified Chinese restaurant located near the Space Needle. Bauhinia's parents, like so many of the parents I've worked with over the years, wanted to make sure that their children were getting the best English and math education possible and that they would thrive academically in this new country.

That same year, our future vice president of IT came to the tutoring center. Victor was a teenager—he'd come in to work on his algebra skills. His family and mine were close—his grandmother had helped Lisa and her brother, Steven, get settled in Seattle—and they had a similar background to ours. He'd arrived a year before we had, in 1988, as a kid of five or six. If you ask him about Vietnam, he has fewer memories, but they're more distinct, more specific to certain events in the way that most kids' memories are. He remembers the heat and humidity, his mom telling him to watch out for bugs because they could make him sick, and being tucked on the platform between the seat and the front of his dad's scooter. He remembers the flash floods, playing outside in the warm rain, and how, in the refugee camp in the Philippines, a man in a strange suit came by to spray their bamboo hut for mosquitoes.

He remembers snippets of the plane ride to the United States, meeting his uncle Alvin at the airport, and driving around and around the infamous spiral ramp coming out of Sea-Tac's parking garage. The first day of school, he and his older sister, Karen, knew no English, and they took the wrong bus. Eventually, however, they found their way.

By the time BrainChild opened, he was fluent in English and most things American. He's always been a quiet person, whip smart, and detail oriented. With me he took the SAT class, and during college at the University of Washington, he began to tutor math at our Bellevue center. He also joined me for other various business ventures, like my foray into real estate and mortgage lending during the boom. As the tutoring business expanded, he stayed right there with me.

Stephanie, too, was part of those early days. She will tell you that she's known me her whole life, and she'll joke that she's known me longer than my own kids have. This is true—she was one of my first students at BrainChild, enrolled by her parents for kindergarten prep. Like many of my students, she was the first generation in her family to be born in the United States. Her parents had arrived in Seattle a few years before she was born, in the 1980s, by way of Guangzhou, China. When she was just a little thing, they'd signed her up for ballet classes at the studio that happened to be located next door to my second tutoring location in Seattle at the Asian Resource Center. Most of her classmates—including Bauhinia and Victor—were also first generation or new arrivals from Vietnam, China, Korea, or India, and like her, many of them stayed at BrainChild throughout their childhoods and beyond. I think this shows a certain kind of Asian mentality when it comes to education—you're not done once you've "caught up." Instead, you're always trying to get ahead and stay ahead. Of course, not only Asians value education in this way; I'm just speaking from my own culture and my own experience.

Stephanie was a cute kid back then, with adorable round cheeks and dark, serious eyes. She grew up fast, as kids do, coming twice a week for math and English classes. In high school, she took BrainChild's SAT prep, and at sixteen, she became a teacher's assistant at the center in Bellevue. While she was attending the University of Washington, she became one of our teachers, then was promoted to manager of the Bellevue center. When she graduated with a degree in accounting and marketing from the Foster School of Business, I immediately hired her to help with marketing and franchising. And the rest is history.

Sometimes when people find out how old my VP of development and finance is, they give me a strange look. Not a lot of people would have hired a recent grad and moved them up so quickly into such an executive role, but Stephanie has always been smart, hardworking, and honest, and because she's grown up in it, she knows the culture, the mission, and the values of the business better than anyone.

Laura, the VP of operations, started from the ground up as well. She's now the business's second-in-command. After graduating from college early, she started as a tutor and has since moved up from there. She's also on the younger end compared to others in the same position, but I could tell right away that she could handle responsibility, and that she really cares about academics and teaching. She's grown into the role beautifully. And I'm excited to see what she can do going forward.

It is fascinating to watch the transition from child to adult, from student to teacher, and I can't help but feel that these people are family. I wholeheartedly agree with Peter Schultz, former CEO of Porsche, who once said, "Hire character. Train skill." I'd add to that: hire potential. From the get-go, I saw the unique potentials of these four individuals, as well as the potentials of the rest of my amazing staff. This is something I pride myself on—the ability to see potential and then provide the environment for it to blossom. Not that I'm the perfect boss—far from it. But I think that this, above all things, is crucial for success.

Together the team works to uphold Best in Class's core values of positivity, energy and passion, adaptability, collaboration, and efficiency, as well as the mission to build better teachers and successful students. Each and every new franchisee is expected to do the same. We provide thorough and in-depth support to our franchisees—beyond the curriculum (which is constantly being updated)—and we offer help with marketing, networking, and technology.

I've traveled all over the world to attend learning events, widen my perspective, and broaden my knowledge in all aspects of life. I've made many friends; we stay connected, share knowledge, and hold one another accountable.

That big belly I got from too much work and stress and food? Gone. I now know that I have to be healthy to be effective, and so I've prioritized eating better and exercising. I think, in the past few years, I've become a kinder, more patient person. I've worked really hard on getting out of the habit of telling people what to do, and I've tried to listen more and be more open-minded to other people's ideas. For so long, I was operating with my nose to the grindstone. Now, I feel like I can lift my head and take a look around. Basically, I've taken my disposition and skills learned through experience, and added some focused training in order to become a better leader. Hopefully, I've become a better father, husband, and son, too. Growing up, I was taught to keep my cards close to my chest, but these days, I want to break that habit and, to the best of my ability, express just how much I appreciate my parents, and how much I love my wife and sons.

On February 14, 2016, to tell the world just how much Lisa means to me, I posted a love letter to her on Facebook.

Thank you, Lisa.

I fell in love with you when we were living in the Philippine refugee camp. I asked you to marry me while I was studying at UBC. I moved to Seattle in May of 1995 and, at that time, I had nothing but a bunch of student loans and you.

I want to take this special day and express my gratitude.

I want to thank you for

- supporting me when I first opened our tutoring business nearly twenty-one years ago—I had no clue what I was getting myself into;
- suffering my bad temper and stubbornness more often than you ought to have;
- supporting me in every decision that I made— even though you did not think it was a good idea and you were right all the time in the end;
- being on my side for every battle in business and life;
- allowing me to make so many mistakes;
- being alongside, supporting, and cheering me up every time I fail;
- always listening without judgment;
- riding your life journey with me although the ride is pretty bumpy;
- taking care of our two wonderful boys while I was on so many business trips;
- planning exciting family trips;
- nourishing my body and soul with home-cooked food;
- being my wonderful lifetime partner and companion.

Thank you, Lisa, for making me the man I am today and giving me your endless love and support in all aspects of my life. I am so grateful to have spent the last twenty-two wonderful years with you, and I am looking forward to spending many more years alongside you. I love you!

Happy Valentine's Day to everyone! I hope this inspires all my friends to express their love to the important people in their lives.

***

Lisa and I took care of each other during that week-long boat ride, and we've tried to take care of each other every day since, no matter the distance between us. All the good things in my life are because of her. And it's because of her that I'm always trying to be a better person.

I've attended the four-day Entrepreneurial Masters Program, hosted by EO and held at MIT, to learn more about leadership and to connect with other entrepreneurs. There, I've had to go deep with some big questions. Last year, our EMP facilitator and current EO global chairman, Brian Brault, emailed me and the other sixty-six members of my cohort with a question: How would you want to be remembered one hundred years from now?

It took me a long time to answer this question, and every day I revisit it to see whether my actions and my answer align. *Why am I here?* I ask myself. *What do I want to contribute? What legacy do I want to leave, and what am I going to do today with that in mind?* When I think—really think—about these questions, it's impossible for me to allow myself to spin my wheels. Instead, I'm able to focus my energy on what matters to me and work day by day toward my goals. As Verne Harnish, the founder of Gazelles

International, says, "Routine sets you free." Everything we do is important. Every moment counts.

A huge percentage of Best in Class's franchise owners, teachers, and students are immigrants or first-generation Americans working to serve the children of their own communities. No surprise there—this country has been built by immigrants, after all. Everyone here is simply trying to make a beautiful life, to seize opportunity and to work hard to put good food on the table, and to give their kids the best education possible so that, when they grow up, they can do the same for their own families. I am proud that my own life has come full circle: I came here with nothing, and I've been able to build a life because of the support and kindness of my family and community. And now I am in a position to do the same for others, offering the same kind of support and kindness. If there's one thing I'm remembered for, I hope it's that.

EPILOGUE

During the schools' Christmas break of 2006, I returned to Vietnam for the first time since my escape eighteen years before. To say that this modern Vietnam was different from the one of my childhood and young adulthood is an understatement. The country I'd left behind had been poor, war-torn, with every person looking over his shoulder and listening at night for a knock on the door. When I arrived with my family all those years later, I looked for signs of that history, of past hunger or sorrow in the faces of passersby. Though all of our stories were different, everyone must have gone through some kind of loss, felt some kind of fear or anger or helplessness, held some kind of painful memory close to their hearts. But the country had moved forward. Evidence of economic development was everywhere. The people on the streets looked healthy and well fed, and they wore bright-colored clothing in good condition. Just like me, the people who'd stayed on in Vietnam seemed to have moved on with their lives. Because that's what you do: you try to survive, and if you do you move on. If you're lucky, like I have been, you have built something worth surviving for. My wife, standing beside me. My boys, who've eaten three well-rounded meals every day of their lives, who've had the best education we could give them.

The house I grew up in was no longer there. I couldn't quite believe it when I arrived at the spot where it had been, only to find a giant concrete slab. I stood there for a while, looking at the pillar holding up the freeway and listening to the sound of cars speeding by above me. I thought about where I'd come from, what I'd lived through, what I'd managed to build. The future.

A week or so into the trip, I had to return home for work. Lisa and the boys stayed on, and for them I'd booked a room at Vinpearl Resort, a recently opened luxury resort on Hon Tre Island, a few hundred miles east of Ho Chi Minh City on Nha Trang Bay. Its sprawling grounds were like those of resorts in Cancun, with palm trees lining the electric-blue pool, and just about every amenity you could imagine. The shopping mall and golf course were just a stone's throw away. At night, the lights illuminated the resort in bright greens and yellows, and by day, the waitstaff moved between the bar and the umbrella-shaded chaise lounges along the beach.

On the flight back to Seattle, I couldn't help but wonder, *What if I had stayed in Vietnam? Would I have built a beautiful life there, too, a life that would have been different from the one I have now but still full and rich in its own way?* The entrepreneurial spirit was in my blood from the start, and had I never escaped, I'm sure I would've made the best of my life in Vietnam. My antenna is always up; I make opportunities wherever I go. Still, America is the land of opportunity, and I am so grateful to live in a free country where everything is transparent, and we can do anything we want as long as it is within the law of the land. I cannot thank this country, our community, and the people around me enough. They have all shaped who I am today. I feel that I am obliged to give back to the community now.

Nothing is impossible if you put your mind, heart, and soul into it. Read every day, visualize your vision every day, and show your gratitude to those around you every day. This is what I know: if you want to build something, you'll build something. It takes laser focus and the ability to keep the future in mind as you organize each day, the ability to weather life's peaks and valleys, and to learn from your mistakes, the resourcefulness to surround yourself with good people who can come together in order to make a great team, and the courage to do what you love.

It is not an easy climb, and every day brings the possibility of both success and failure. And that unpredictability, that open question that starts each day, is what makes it fun, and worth it.

ACKNOWLEDGMENTS

I would like to express my sincerest gratitude to my coach Ron Huntington, for being a pillar of advice and inspiration throughout the entire process of creating this book. I will forever be indebted to you for the beautiful words you provided for the foreword. Your reassuring guidance has helped me stay focused and prosperous, and has also done so for my family, my team, and my businesses. Thank you for your ongoing support and friendship.

I want to thank Ted Tanase, who has been my good friend and mentor for the past three years. You have helped in so many different areas of my life, and I could not be the happy person I am today without you. I am also extremely grateful that you brought Sue McNab into my life. Sue, you have been a tremendous help keeping me and my team on track and focused on the bigger picture. You are someone I never hesitate to reach out to when I encounter a problem, and it is fortuitous to have someone like that in my life.

None of this would be possible without the support, encouragement, and hard-working attitudes of my Best in Class team. From the executive team to the franchisees to the managers, directors, and staff, everyone was willing to work above and beyond so that I would have time to work on this book. I am very grateful for their support and dedication to me, to the company, and in marketing this book to the masses. This is a unique group of individuals capable of moving mountains! Best in Class Education Center would not be where it is today without every single one of them.

I appreciate all the hard work that Anna Katz and Emilie Sandoz-Voyer at Girl Friday Productions have put toward getting this book developed over the past year. Anna, I commend you for your extreme professionalism, constant flexibility, and forgiving patience with me when having to reschedule so many times. Emilie, thank you for your sense of urgency and attention to detail in getting everything wrapped up in a timely manner to meet our ever-changing deadlines.

I want to send a special thank-you to all of my good friends and affiliates with Entrepreneurs' Organization (EO). This extraordinary group has allowed me to flourish within my community—professionally, personally, and with my family as well. I am honored to have had the opportunity to serve on the board of the EO Seattle Chapter and Forum and value the support the members of that organization have provided toward the book efforts.

My sincere appreciation goes out to all those who read early versions of the manuscript and provided feedback and encouragement. In particular, I would also like to express my deep gratitude to the writers, business leaders, mentors, and colleagues who took the time to read the book and found it worthwhile enough to offer the words of praise included on the cover and in the interior of this book. Thank you for your time, energy, and insights.

I am grateful for the support of my entire family. I would like to thank my parents, Tham Lam and Nhuan Chau, for all their hard work in raising me and enduring my antics when I was a kid, and for forgiving me when I was a disappointment during my teenage years. You both instilled values in me that I still carry to this day. I am a hard worker thanks to the example my father showed me all my life, and I am certain that my passion for teaching stems from my mother's commitment to education back in Vietnam.

I want to thank my younger sister, Kitty Lam Do, for dealing with me her entire life, especially when we were little and I would constantly beat her up. Your consistent love and support for me and my family through the ups and downs of our life has been immeasurable. Your willingness to work alongside me—not only with Best in Class, but also in our real estate, restaurant, and other business ventures as well—has brought us closer than I ever knew we could be. So many wonderful opportunities have been made available to us, and I am forever beholden to you for the altruistic love you show me and my family.

Thank you to my sons, Louis and Albert, whom I love dearly. I have learned so much from both of you. You are the reason I get up in the morning, so I can focus on building a better life for you and your future families. Thank you for putting up with me when I was too busy to spend quality time with you. I am extremely grateful for your understanding, and for your willingness to be present when we could find the time to be together.

Most importantly, to Lisa, the love of my life—there are no words to express how truly appreciative I am for all the blood, sweat, and tears that you have shared with me throughout our crazy life together. Thank you so much for supporting me and my outrageous goals, even in those times you foresaw difficulties and a tough road ahead. I could not have asked for a more perfect partner to build a family with and stand alongside through this amazing life.

ABOUT THE AUTHOR

© Benz Photography

Hao Lam is the owner of Best in Class Education Center, a franchise of education centers devoted to the success of teachers, students, and franchisees. Founded in 2010, Best in Class is synonymous with passion for education and investment in community, supporting teachers and franchisees in their individual growth, helping students achieve academic excellence, and giving franchisees the chance to live the American dream. Lam currently lives in Seattle with his family.

Made in the USA
Lexington, KY
29 April 2018